PRAYER
THE ULTIMATE CONVERSATION

CHARLES F. STANLEY

PRAYER
THE ULTIMATE CONVERSATION

Originally published as *The Ultimate Conversation*

HOWARD BOOKS
A DIVISION OF SIMON & SCHUSTER, INC.
New York • Nashville • London • Toronto • Sydney • New Delhi

Howard Books
A Division of Simon & Schuster, Inc.
1230 Avenue of the Americas
New York, NY 10020

This book was previously published in 2012 as *The Ultimate Conversation*.

First Howard Books trade paperback edition May 2013

HOWARD and colophon are trademarks of Simon & Schuster, Inc.

For information about special discounts for bulk purchases, please contact Simon & Schuster Special Sales at 1-866-506-1949 or business@simonandschuster.com.

The Simon & Schuster Speakers Bureau can bring authors to your live event. For more information or to book an event, contact the Simon & Schuster Speakers Bureau at 1-866-248-3049 or visit our website at www.simonspeakers.com.

Manufactured in the United States of America

10   9

Library of Congress Cataloging-in-Publication data is available.

ISBN 978-1-4391-9065-4
ISBN 978-1-4516-6860-5 (pbk)
ISBN 978-1-4516-2885-2 (ebook)

Of all the lessons I have learned from my dad, of all the challenges I have seen him face, of all the successes I have helped him celebrate, of all the disappointments I know he has suffered, the characteristic that defines him most is his relationship with God through prayer. Nothing has influenced me more than observing his daily habit of meeting with God behind closed doors, on his knees, Bible open, and with little regard for time.

—BECKY STANLEY BRODERSEN, APRIL 2012

CONTENTS

Contents

PRAYER
THE ULTIMATE CONVERSATION

1

A CONVERSATION WITH THE GREAT PROBLEM SOLVER

Your Priceless Privilege

DID YOU KNOW THAT YOU are the beneficiary of a great honor? You have the *privilege* of coming into the very throne room of the Great I AM. Not only have you been invited to stand in His presence, you have been invited to *conversation,* an intimate dialogue with the One who cares about you most. It is the ultimate conversation: your opportunity to seek understanding from your Creator; your chance to ask the Lord of all that exists to deliver you in the areas where you cannot help yourself; and your privilege to know Him better.

People read books about prayer for all kinds of reasons. Some want to be sure they face life in the most positive and effective way possible. They know the Father will lead them in the very best paths for their lives, so they strive to learn the practical aspects of communicating with Him.

Others find themselves in situations where they have no other option than to look to God for guidance. The challenges they face are so far beyond their abilities that they realize they cannot rescue themselves. They recognize they need the Savior and long for Him to deliver them from their difficulties and sufferings.

Prayer is an intimate dialogue with the One who cares about you most.

At times, people struggle with the question "Why?" so intensely that they don't know where else to turn for answers. They hope the Lord will, in some way, give their lives significance and meaning.

Some simply want to know God intimately, personally, and profoundly—and that is a wonderful reason to pray. In fact, learning about the Father and understanding His ways should motivate our times of communion with Him. He loves us and wants us to know Him.

Whatever your goal for reading this book about the ultimate conversation, I want to encourage you to seek the Lord and go to the throne of grace more frequently, with greater intensity and focus. It is at His throne that you will discover life at its very best—a life characterized and enriched by a growing, vibrant relationship with the Lord God Almighty, the Great Problem Solver.

A CONVERSATION? REALLY?

Perhaps you are wondering if a conversation with the God of the Universe is really possible. After all, most people say they pray, but when you press them about whether they truly believe the Lord hears and answers them, they reply, "I hope so." They may not have confidence that He will respond because they don't really trust His character. They may doubt they are worthy of His attention.

Let me assure you, God never intended us to approach Him with a "hope so" attitude. He wants us to *trust* Him. Our good, loving, and powerful heavenly Father is always available to hear and answer the prayers of His children. His response to us may not be what we expect, but He never fails to reply if we're willing to listen.

So when people ask me if I really believe that a conversation with God is actually possible, I can answer truthfully, "Yes, I absolutely do." In Jeremiah 33:3 He promises, "Call to Me and I will answer you, and I will tell you great and mighty things, which you do not know." The Lord has never gone back on a promise, and He never will (Josh. 21:45; 1 Kings 8:56). We can trust Him to answer us (Ps. 91:15).

This brings us to the first foundational principle of this book:

FOUNDATIONAL PRINCIPLE #1

God *desires* to communicate with us.

We must start here, because as Hebrews 11:6 tells us, "He who comes to God must believe that He is and that He is a rewarder of those who seek Him." The Father wants you to know Him in a profound way and walk in intimate fellowship with Him.

Your Opportunity for Personal Relationship with God

I can say this because I've experienced a deeply personal relationship with Him. As I reflect on my life, I can recount many long, connected seasons of nearly constant prayer, talking with the Father at every opportunity. At times His presence was so powerful that all I could do was whisper praises to His holy name in awe and wonder. Sometimes the pain was so deep and my helplessness so overwhelming, I could only cry out to Him in desperation. I have experienced both moments of weeping and seasons of joy before His throne. He has never disappointed or abandoned me—not once (Deut. 31:8, 16; Heb. 13:5).

The Father wants you to know Him in a profound way and walk in intimate fellowship with Him.

You, too, can know so constant a Helper, so faithful a Friend, so worthy a Warrior, so wise a Leader, and so great a Redeemer. You, too, can experience God as deeply and intimately as I have because He is so absolutely wonderful.

The best part is, you don't need anything extra to enjoy His love and wisdom—just an open heart that hungers to know Him. I know a dear lady who has a seat in her sewing room that she calls her "God chair." She sits there only to pray—not for any other purpose. Daily she goes there to seek the Father, often for an hour or more at a time. It is her special place whenever she desires to experience the Lord's presence. Is there anything extraordinary, supernatural, or important about that chair? No. It is simply an old chair. But it represents her communion with the living God and the fact that there is absolutely nothing better than knowing Him.

YOUR PRICELESS PRIVILEGE

Why am I so passionate about talking to the Father? Because I want you to enjoy the very best life possible. And if you've ever spent time with God, perhaps you've experienced how energizing and encouraging His presence can be.

I am constantly amazed at the insights and principles the Father shows me in His Word during periods of quiet, prayerful meditation. When I've had to face painful trials, His loving comfort and guidance have helped me emerge stronger in spirit and victorious, rather than weaker and defeated. And I can only attribute anything productive or effective in my ministry to His wisdom and power.

Is that what you desire: Deep insight and understanding? Comfort and guidance that help you triumph in your trials? Wisdom and power that lead you to success in life? These are the rewards of a vibrant, steadfast, continuing conversation with God.

You see, you and I have been given a great privilege in

prayer, and the Lord desires that we receive and use this gift every day of our lives. However, we must realize that though this honor is free to us, it was costly to God.

This brings us to the second foundational principle:

FOUNDATIONAL PRINCIPLE #2

Prayer is rooted in a *personal relationship* with God.
Its purpose is to *strengthen and deepen* your intimacy
    with Him.

Our conversation with God is the way in which we grow closer to Him. But if you and I don't have relationships with the Lord to begin with, then our prayers will be powerless. How do we enter into relationships with the Father? It is very simple, and it all begins with Jesus (John 14:6; Rom. 5:1).

The truth is, you and I cannot know God until we first allow His Son, Jesus Christ, to reconcile us to Him.

Colossians 1:20–22 tells us:

It was the Father's good pleasure for all the fullness to dwell in Him [Jesus], and through Him to reconcile all things to Himself, having made peace through the blood of His cross; through Him, I say, whether things on earth or things in heaven. And although you were formerly alienated and hostile in mind, engaged in evil deeds, yet He has now reconciled you in His fleshly body through death, in order to present you before Him holy and blameless and beyond reproach.

JESUS RECONCILES US TO THE FATHER

We are all separated from the Lord because of our sinfulness (Rom. 3:23). But through His death on the cross and His resurrection, Jesus forgave us of our sins and restored our ability to have eternal, everlasting relationships with the Father. As I said, our privilege of an ongoing conversation with God was very costly but is an awesome gift that can never be lost.

What does salvation through Jesus accomplish for us? His redemption means that you and I never have to feel unworthy when approaching the Lord. We never have to feel shame in God's presence when we know Jesus as our Savior. We are absolutely forgiven, completely cleansed of all we've ever done wrong.

> *We never have to feel shame in God's presence when we know Jesus as our Savior.*

Psalm 103:12 promises, "As far as the east is from the west, so far has He removed our transgressions from us." Romans 8:1 also confirms, "There is now no condemnation for those who are in Christ Jesus." He loves us and always welcomes us as "holy and blameless and beyond reproach" (Col. 1:22).

You may be thinking, *I've never trusted Jesus as my Savior. I've never entered into a relationship with God. But I would like to.*

It is not difficult; Jesus has done all the work for you. All you need to do is accept His provision by faith (Eph. 2:8–9). Acknowledge that you have sinned and ask Him to forgive you. You can tell Him in your own words or use this simple prayer:

Lord Jesus, I ask You to forgive my sins and save me from eternal separation from God. By faith, I accept Your work and death on the cross as sufficient payment for my sins. Thank You for providing the way for me to know You and to have a relationship with my heavenly Father. Through faith in You, I have eternal life and can enjoy the ultimate conversation. Thank You for hearing my prayers and loving me unconditionally. Please give me the strength, wisdom, and determination to walk in the center of Your will. In Jesus' name, I pray. Amen.

I can still remember the Sunday I came to know Jesus as my very own personal Savior. I accepted God as my Redeemer at the age of twelve, and I recall sitting in church with my buddies Clyde, James, Tig, and Nelson. A lady was preaching that morning, so my friends and I got there early and sat on the second row.

Normally I was a little distracted when we all sat together, but this morning was different. When she finished talking and the organ began to play, I did not feel right on the inside.

I suddenly felt lonely and disconnected from my friends. Even more disturbing, I felt isolated from my mom, the only person I had in the world. But worst of all, I realized that I was separated from God, too.

I did not know the Father at all at that point. I knew *about* Him, but He was not in me like He was in my mom. I did not have the faith she had. All the nights we knelt by my bed, I had relied on her prayers to be answered, not mine. I had even gone to Sunday school long enough to know that I was going to hell when I died and I would never see my mom or my friends again. But finally, during this church service, the true nature of my condemnation dawned on me.

It was no use fighting the tears. More frightened than embarrassed, I asked Clyde and Tig to step aside as I made my way to the aisle. I walked to the front of the sanctuary as fast as I could and knelt at the altar to pray. As I began to repent of my sin and ask Jesus into my heart I noticed that my friends had followed and had formed a circle around me. The more I cried, the lighter I felt. The heavy weight of my sin and guilt was gone. I had received Jesus in exchange, and He was lighter than a sack of newspapers.

I pray that if you are carrying the full burden of your sin, you will do as I did—go before you heavenly Father, confess your transgressions, and allow Him to free you.

ARE YOU LISTENING?

Once you have a relationship with Jesus, the Holy Spirit indwells you (Eph. 1:13–14). John 14:26 describes His role in us: "The Helper, the Holy Spirit, whom the Father will send in My name, He will teach you all things, and bring to your remembrance all that I said to you." His goal is to reveal the Lord's ways—communicating God's will and enabling you to accomplish all He calls you to do.

He encourages you to share your heart with God, but also directs you to pay attention to what the Father is teaching you.

The Holy Spirit strengthens your intimacy with the Father by continually drawing you into His presence. However, He does not usher you to the throne of grace simply so you can give the Lord a list of demands. He is there to *deepen* your relationship. This means He encourages you to share your heart with God, but also directs you to pay attention to what the Father is teaching you.

This brings us to our final foundational principle:

FOUNDATIONAL PRINCIPLE #3

The ultimate conversation is not just about you talking
    to God.
To truly interact with Him, you must *listen* to Him
    as well.

If you desire to experience the ultimate conversation, you must be an active listener, purposefully seeking the Father's will and doing as He says. Deuteronomy 4:29–31 promises, "You will seek the LORD your God, and you will find Him if you search for Him with all your heart and all your soul. When you are in distress . . . return to the LORD your God and listen to His voice. For the LORD your God is a compassionate God; He will not fail you."

How do we actively listen to God? People often ask me how they can pray better. I've realized what they are really asking is: *How can we get to the place where we know God's voice and have the confidence to follow Him?*

Perhaps this is what you would like to learn as well. Do you want to understand how you can know God, grow in your relationship with Him, and find greater fulfillment in your life? Do you long to hear His voice, to experience His wisdom, comfort, power, guidance, and love as you face a difficult challenge or trial? Do you yearn for an active, meaningful, ongoing conversation with the Lord of all creation, one that will continue into eternity?

I hope so, because these are the questions we will explore in the following pages. We will also examine similar topics such as:

- Why you can trust God's character as you speak with Him
- The importance of listening to His voice
- The things that can hinder you from hearing Him

- How the Holy Spirit helps you pray
- How to win your battles on your knees
- How to pray for others
- God's ultimate goal in speaking with you

I hope you will be blessed by this book and grow deeper in your relationship with the Lord. With this in mind, I pray:

Father, how grateful we are that You desire to communicate with us. Thank You for reconciling us to Yourself through the death and resurrection of Your Son, Jesus Christ, and for giving us the awesome privilege of prayer to strengthen and deepen our relationships with You. I also thank You for Your Holy Spirit who indwells each and every believer—teaching us how to listen to You and enabling us to do Your will.

Father, I pray especially for this reader who desires to communicate with You and know You better. God, draw this one into an intimate relationship with Yourself, teaching this individual how to connect with You in deeper, more meaningful ways than ever before. Help Your child to be open, yielded, and available for whatever You desire to do. Thank You for revealing Your ways and for making Yourself known to this soul.

To You be all the honor, glory, power, and praise. In Jesus' matchless name, I pray. Amen.

2

⌁

WITH WHOM ARE
YOU SPEAKING?

Your Perception of God Will Characterize
Your Prayer Life

WHY DO I SAY THAT prayer is the ultimate conversation?
What makes it so powerful and impactful? It is not prayer
itself that holds the power; it is the God to whom we pray.

So let me ask you: What do you suppose God is like?
What characteristics do you associate with
Him? Do you believe the Father is big
enough—sufficiently powerful, wise, and
loving—to handle all the challenges you
bring to Him? Are you absolutely confident that He *can* help you and also that
He *will*? How you view God has immense
ramifications for both your prayer life and
your relationship with Him.

> *It is not prayer
> itself that holds
> the power; it
> is the God to
> whom we pray.*

A friend of mine knew a man who had turned his back
on God. He lived according to his own lusts and desires, his

life filled with immoral behaviors and addictions. Eventually, he became seriously ill. My friend tried to minister to him, but the man would not acknowledge that there could be an authority higher than his own will. Seeing the man without hope and deteriorating in health quickly, my friend suggested that he pray about his troubles. The man relented, deciding he would do so as a last resort. However, he confided, "I'm not sure who is on the other end of the line when I pray."

"Well, God is," my friend replied, hoping it would comfort him.

"Oh, no!" this man exclaimed. "I can't possibly pray to God."

"Really?" my friend asked, taken aback. "Well, then to whom do you think you would be praying?"

"I'd probably just be talking to myself," the man replied cynically. Then he added, "Like *that* is going to do me any good. If I knew how to make myself well, I wouldn't need to talk to myself about it!"

How heartbreaking! This man had lived life as if he were the ultimate authority and the most important opinion. Yet when he truly needed help—when he could not save himself—he could not overcome his self-focused perspective. He limited himself to his own resources and faults rather than trusting the One who is all-knowing, all-powerful, ever-present, and completely loving.

Sadly, we may be guilty of the same thing. Although we may acknowledge that God exists and praise Him for His attributes, perhaps we try to resolve difficulties ourselves rather than taking them to Him—the Great Problem Solver. When we pray, do we have our own limitations in mind? From our narrow, earthbound points of view, perhaps we see no hope in our situations, no solutions to our dilemmas, and no end to our sufferings. So when we go before Him, do we come dejected and doubting, questioning His goodness for allowing us to endure trials? If so, we are like the man in the story: talking to ourselves about circumstances we cannot change.

Instead, when we approach God, we must embrace the fact that we are interacting with the Almighty, our Lord, Maker, King, Mighty Warrior, Redeemer, and faithful High Priest. After all, trusting God means looking beyond what we can see to what He sees and can accomplish.

The Father proclaims, "Behold, I am the LORD, the God of all flesh; is anything too difficult for Me?" (Jer. 32:37). No, there is absolutely *nothing* too challenging for Him to overcome! But how can you and I know this for certain?

I AM WHO I AM

The truth is, we can know who God is because He never changes. He has been consistent, unwavering, and absolutely faithful throughout history. As Hebrews 13:8 reminds us, "Jesus Christ *is* the same yesterday and today and forever." His character does not differ in His dealings from one person to another, or from one era to the next. He is the one perfect, unfaltering standard of goodness, holiness, justice, and loving-kindness.

The Father demonstrated this in an incredible way during His encounter with Moses at the burning bush. He called the shepherd to deliver Israel from Egyptian bondage—a task far greater, immensely more complicated, and abundantly more difficult than anything Moses could ever hope to achieve on his own.

So the Lord comforted Moses by revealing His identity to him: "I am the God of your father, the God of Abraham, the God of Isaac, and the God of Jacob" (Ex. 3:6). Everything that He did for Abraham, Isaac, and Jacob, He would also do for Moses.

Although the statement was powerful, it was not enough for Moses, who was facing a task that would cause any of us to tremble. Delivering Israel put him at odds not only with Pharaoh but also with the entire Egyptian army. And Moses had no forces of his own to help. Also, there was no guarantee that the people of Israel would trust him enough to follow.

So Moses asked, "Behold, I am going to the sons of Israel, and I will say to them, 'The God of your fathers has sent me to you.' Now they may say to me, 'What is His name?' What shall I say to them?" (Ex. 3:13).

The Lord graciously replied in a manner that would be unmistakable to Moses. He said, "I AM WHO I AM . . . Thus you shall say to the sons of Israel, 'I AM has sent me to you' " (Ex. 3:14).

Unfortunately, the English language sometimes fails to capture the awesome power of God's Word. We read that the Lord says, "I AM WHO I AM," but the Hebrew carries a deeper, more timeless meaning. It can be translated as "I Will Always Be Who I Have Always Been," indicating that God will forever be who He has been from eternity.

Thus He was telling Moses that the Creator who formed the heavens, earth, stars, skies, and all that exists would use His unfathomable power to help him succeed.

God will forever be who He has been from eternity.

The living Lord who molded mankind from the dust of the earth would skillfully design a way for Moses to triumph against Pharaoh and his army.

The God who cleansed the world with a flood, and yet kept His servant Noah safe, would guard Moses' life regardless of the dangers.

The Covenant Keeper who miraculously created the nation of Israel from one-hundred-year-old Abraham's offspring would not fail in delivering His people from Egyptian bondage.

And the great Deliverer who never abandoned Joseph, but raised him up so Israel could be saved, would be with Moses and accomplish even greater feats through him.

ANSWERS TO QUESTIONS ABOUT
GOD'S CHARACTER

The best news is that the God who helped Moses and who has actively delivered His people throughout history is available to you today. This is how you can be certain of His character, attributes, and love for you: He hasn't changed and never will.

Because we know His nature is both eternal and consistent, we can answer some of the other questions that arise when we consider having a conversation with Him:

- Can I truly trust God?
- Does the Father really have the ability to help me?
- Is the Lord genuinely willing to listen to me and come to my aid?

So let us answer these issues by exploring some of His qualities and seeing who invites us to communicate with Him.

Can I Truly Trust God?

One of my favorite passages of Scripture, Proverbs 3:5–6, instructs, "Trust in the LORD with all your heart and do not lean on your own understanding. In all your ways acknowledge Him, and He will make your paths straight." But what makes God trustworthy? Why should you and I place our faith in His character?

You and I can count on the Lord because of His steadfast

holiness and unassailable integrity (Num. 23:19; Ps. 22:3–4). People in your life may disappoint you. They may not always be honest or act in your best interest. But you can be certain the Father will do what is good, loving, and righteous on your behalf because He is *holy* and always does the right thing.

The God who helped Moses and who has actively delivered His people throughout history is available to you today.

Hebrews 6:18 promises, "It is impossible for God to lie." When the Father says He cares for you, it is not a trick; it is the absolute truth. He will never lead you astray but will always be honorable and guide you in the best way possible.

So *yes*, you can trust the Lord's wonderful character.

Does the Father Really Have the Ability to Help Me?

Of course, the value of any promise is based not only on the character of the person making the guarantee but also on His capacity to fulfill it. Let me assure you, God has *never* failed to keep His word. Solomon proclaimed in 1 Kings 8:56, "Blessed be the Lord . . . not one word has failed of all His good promise." He is absolutely capable—wise, strong, and loving—of fulfilling your needs, no matter how overwhelming they may seem.

This is because our God is *sovereign;* He is the majestic Ruler of all creation. He set the laws of nature in place. Matter, space, and time are in His hand and under His authority.

Psalm 103:19 tells us, "The LORD has established His throne in the heavens, and His sovereignty rules over all."

God is absolutely capable—wise, strong, and loving—of fulfilling your needs, no matter how overwhelming they may seem.

What this means for your situation is that the Father is *omnipotent*—He is all-powerful. He can literally move heaven and earth to accomplish His will for you because He put them in place and guides their every movement (Ps. 104).

Also, the Lord is *omniscient*, which signifies He is all-knowing and completely wise. He sees your past, present, and future and understands everything about your situation, even details you could not possibly discern. He identifies exactly what you need and how to provide it, but He also recognizes how to best use your difficulties to build you up and mature your faith (Rom. 8:28).

Additionally, God is *omnipresent*. He is outside of time and everywhere at once, so He is always with you in every moment, no matter where you go (Josh. 1:9). Nothing in your life escapes His notice. He is able to rally resources and influence circumstances that you don't even know exist in order to solve the problems you're facing, regardless of what they are.

Luke 1:37 testifies, "Nothing will be impossible with God." No matter how deep, wide, piercing, mighty, complicated, or overwhelming the trials you face, the living Lord is greater and can lead you to victory in them (John 16:33). So again the response is *yes*, the Father is really *able* to help you.

Is the Lord Genuinely Willing to Listen to Me and Come to My Aid?

Here is the question many of us struggle to answer. Although we may accept that God is trustworthy and capable of delivering us from our troubles, we are not quite certain that He is *willing* to do so. These doubts often stem from feelings of inadequacy: We doubt we are worthy of His love and presence.

First, understand that the Lord accepts us based on Christ's death on the cross, not because of what we've done or have failed to do (Eph. 2:8–9). As I said in the previous chapter, you and I can have relationships with the Father only through the salvation Jesus provides. However, once we trust Christ as our Savior, we are always able to approach the throne of grace (Heb. 4:14–16). Jude 1:24 promises that Jesus "is able to keep you from stumbling, and to make you stand in the presence of His glory blameless with great joy." You don't have to feel shame or unworthiness before the Father—Jesus took care of your shame on the cross. He is your adequacy. Of course, you should always repent of your sins, but that is to keep your fellowship with God unhindered, not so you can earn His approval.

Second, understand that as well as being omnipotent, omniscient, and omnipresent, the Father is also *omni-benevolent*, which means He is unconditional and perfect in His love for you. The Lord's love isn't based on what you do—it is based on His own unfailing character. First John 4:8–10 explains, "God is love. By this the love of God was manifested in us, that God has sent His only begotten Son into the world so that we might live through Him. In this is love, not that we loved God, but that He loved us and sent His Son to be the propitiation for our sins."

This means the Father is completely kind and compassionate toward us because He cannot be otherwise. Everything He does is motivated by His care for us and is ultimately meant to bring us joy and fulfillment.

There is no need to wonder if the Lord is *willing* to help you—He is! Romans 8:31–32 declares, "What then shall we say to these things? If God is for us, who is against us? He who did not spare His own Son, but delivered Him over for us all, how will He not also with Him freely give us all things?"

The Father sometimes allows difficulties in your life just so you will recognize your need for Him. Not only is God prepared to help you; He is actively calling you to cast "all your anxiety on Him, because He cares for you" (1 Pet. 5:7).

Why Is My View of God So Crucial to My Prayer Life?

Now, perhaps you are wondering how practical all of this is. How can trusting God's character change your situations and circumstances? Why is *how* you see Him so important to your prayer life?

First, your opinion of the Lord influences your attitude in talking to Him. If you have a low view of the Father— thinking He is not actively engaged in your life or that He is in some way cruel—then you won't want to interact with

Him. No one wants to spend time with people who are indifferent or mean.

However, if you love and respect Him as God Almighty—realizing the great privilege you have in being able to converse with Him—then you'll want to approach His throne with humility and expectancy. We're motivated to be near those we value highly. We want to learn from them and express our appreciation. We recognize that the opportunities to be around them are a gift. The same is true in our relationships with God.

> *Not only is God prepared to help you; He is actively calling you to cast "all your anxiety on Him, because He cares for you."* (1 Pet. 5:7)

Second, your view of the Lord affects the nature of your prayers. Have you ever examined the substance of your conversations with the Father? What you express during your time alone with the Lord will tell you a great deal about what you think of Him. It will also explain your enthusiasm or reluctance to enter into His presence.

Are you going before the Lord to know and worship Him? Or do you list all the things you would like Him to do? Are you seeking His will because you know His ways are best? Or do you bring Him your plans, hoping He'll bless them? Are your prayers self-centered or God-centered?

If you're consistently focused on yourself during times with the Lord, then your attention is misplaced. You are missing out on one of the greatest blessings a soul can experience—the love and power of being in His awesome presence.

Third, your perception of the Father impacts whether or not you really expect Him to answer you. Hebrews 11:6 is clear: "Without faith it is impossible to please Him, for he who comes to God must believe that He is and that He is a rewarder of those who seek Him." Do you trust the Lord is working on your behalf? Are you confident He hears your petitions and is leading you in the best way possible? If not, you may be like the man in the story at the beginning of this chapter—just talking to yourself.

But to the person who believes God is able, who prays according to His will, and who walks in an intimate relationship with Him, Jesus says, "All things for which you pray and ask, believe that you have received them, and they will be *granted* you" (Mark 11:24).

Putting It into Practice: The Story of Nehemiah

We are now going to examine the life of a man who talked to the Lord during a very dark and difficult time in history: Nehemiah, the cupbearer to King Artaxerxes I of Persia. Although he was facing terrible circumstances, Nehemiah's prayers clearly exhibited his absolute confidence in the Father's trustworthy character, ability, and willingness to help him. Before we get to Nehemiah's prayer, it's important that we first recall what was happening in history and how this servant of God ended up a citizen of Persia. What follows is a simple chart to help you follow along with the timeline.

A Brief History

c. 605 B.C.	Babylonian invasion and first deportation from Jerusalem
c. 597 B.C.	Second deportation of Judahites to Babylon
c. 586 B.C.	Third deportation and destruction of Temple and Jerusalem
c. 539 B.C.	Cyrus II of Persia overthrows Babylonian Empire
c. 538 B.C.	Cyrus decrees that Jews can return to Jerusalem
c. 537 B.C.	Jews begin returning to Jerusalem to rebuild Temple
c. 515 B.C.	Second Temple completed
c. 465 B.C.	Artaxerxes I ascends to the throne of Persia
c. 445 B.C.	Nehemiah prays for God's help to restore Jerusalem's walls

From 605 B.C. to 586 B.C., King Nebuchadnezzar's forces took the Jewish people captive, deporting them from Judah and exiling them throughout the lands of the Babylonian Empire (2 Kings 24:10–16). It was a terrible time for the people, separated from their homes and loved ones. They were forced to adjust to a culture that was very different from their own.

However, they had cause for hope. God promised them that their banishment to Babylon would not last forever. They would once again return to the land of their inheritance. Jeremiah wrote:

Thus says the LORD of hosts, the God of Israel, to all the exiles whom I have sent into exile from Jerusalem to Babylon, "Build houses and live in them; and plant gardens and eat their produce. . . . *When seventy years have been completed for Babylon, I will visit you and fulfill My good word to you, to bring you back to this place* [Jerusalem]. . . . I will be found by you," declares the LORD, "and I will restore your fortunes and will gather you from all the nations and from all the places where I have driven you," declares the LORD, "and I will bring you back to the place from where I sent you into exile." (Jer. 29:4–5, 10, 14, emphasis added)

Just as the Lord promised, when the seventy years neared completion, He set the stage to send the people of Judah home. This plan included the Medo-Persians overthrowing the Babylonian Empire and taking over their lands, which meant they became the new overseers of the captive Jews.

Then something miraculous happened. God caused one of the Persian monarchs to take pity on the Judahites and write a history-changing proclamation. King Cyrus declared:

The LORD, the God of heaven, has given me all the kingdoms of the earth and He has appointed me to build Him a house in Jerusalem, which is in Judah. Whoever there is among you of all His people, may his God be with him! Let him go up to Jerusalem which is in Judah and rebuild the house of the LORD, the God of Israel; He is the God who is in Jerusalem. (Ezra 1:2–3)

Finally, the people of Judah were permitted to return home (circa 537 B.C.). What they found there was terribly disheartening. The Babylonians had devastated the region, especially the capital of Jerusalem. The walls had been toppled and the temple destroyed, leaving nothing of the city's former glory (2 Kings 25:8–11). It seemed that the land of their inheritance would never recover.

The story of Nehemiah begins more than ninety years later (circa 445 B.C.) in the city of Susa. This godly man served as cupbearer under Persian King Artaxerxes I, who reigned from circa 465 B.C. to 425 B.C. Artaxerxes counted on Nehemiah to ensure that his wine was safe to drink and free of poisons. Because of this loyal and trusted service, Nehemiah had some influence with the king.

A devout Jew, Nehemiah heard that his brother Hanani and others from Judah had arrived at the king's palace. He sought them out for news about the conditions in Jerusalem. He had cause for concern. Just a few years earlier, Israel's enemies convinced Artaxerxes that the people were readying themselves for rebellion, so the king commanded that any rebuilding of Jerusalem's walls cease (Ezra 4:8–23). Unprotected, the city was constantly in danger.

What Nehemiah heard broke his heart—the situation was

far worse than he expected: "They said to me, 'The remnant there in the province who survived the captivity are in great distress and reproach, and the wall of Jerusalem is broken down and its gates are burned with fire.' When I heard these words, I sat down and wept and mourned for days; and I was fasting and praying before the God of heaven" (Neh. 1:3–4).

Nehemiah was in prayer night and day for an extended period of time. Even as he went about his responsibilities in the palace, he was in constant conversation with the Lord.

The God Whom He Served

Although he faced an overwhelming situation, Nehemiah prayed. The first thing we should note in Nehemiah's prayer is how deeply he believed in the Lord, which we can assess through how he addressed Him (Neh. 1:5–11). You see, in ancient times, names carried significant meaning because they revealed one's character.

Nehemiah said: "I beseech You, LORD God of heaven, the *great* and *awesome* God, who preserves the covenant and loving-kindness for those who love Him and keep His commandments . . . O *Lord,* I beseech You, may Your ear be attentive to the prayer of Your servant and the prayer of Your servants who delight to revere Your name" (Neh. 1:5, 11, emphasis added).

We can tell a great deal about God's nature by examining the Hebrew names Nehemiah used to call out to Him.

1. Nehemiah Addressed Him as YHWH (v. 5).

Have you ever wondered what it means when you see "LORD" in all capitals in your Bible? Why is He represented this way in Scripture? This presentation of God's proper name indicates a specific word in the original Hebrew that we transliterate as *YHWH*. Because these four letters do not include vowels, we aren't certain of the exact pronunciation, though *Yahweh* and *Jehovah* are commonly used.

He is the existing One—the "I AM" who brings all things into being.

This wondrous name means that He is the existing One—the "I AM" who brings all things into being—and it is found more than 6,500 times in the Old Testament. Just as Moses learned at the burning bush, Nehemiah understood that the One he addressed is the unchanging, preexistent Lord who set the universe in place. YHWH miraculously brought the nation of Israel into existence, and He could restore it to its former glory as well. The Father had always been and would always be the unfailing God of love, grace, mercy, and justice who could accomplish the impossible on behalf of His people.

2. Nehemiah Addressed Him as Elohim (v. 5).

Paired with "LORD," Nehemiah used the word "God," which is *Elohim* in Hebrew. *Elohim* is found more than 2,600 times throughout Scripture and comes from a root that means "deity, strength, power, and might." It can also signify "Creator,

Preserver, One who is Mighty and Strong" and "to swear, make a covenant, or keep a pledge." So when we read the name Elohim, we are seeing the One who is infinite in power and absolutely faithful to keep His promises to us. We can be confident that He will always fulfill His plans for our lives.

Although Nehemiah was helpless to improve the situation in Jerusalem, he knew that the omnipotent, omniscient, omnipresent, and omni-benevolent Lord could. Not only could God restore Jerusalem, but Nehemiah was confident He would be unfalteringly faithful to the covenants He had made with Abraham and David.

3. Nehemiah Addressed Him as Adonai (v. 11).

The last name Nehemiah called out in his prayer to the Almighty was "Lord," which is *Adonai* in Hebrew. Nehemiah acknowledged Him as Master—the ultimate Ruler over all things, whose authority and power are infinite (Ps. 103:19). However, the word *Adonai* also carries with it the understanding that the Owner is responsible for the provision, protection, and guidance of those under His care.

All kingdoms are in the hand of the Lord, and all monarchs subject to His sovereignty. Although Nehemiah was merely a servant in the eyes of Artaxerxes, he served the God who governed the ruler. As Proverbs 21:1 explains, "The king's heart is like channels of water in the hand of the LORD; He turns it wherever He wishes." Just as Adonai had raised the Persians to defeat the Babylonians, He could convince Artaxerxes to help Nehemiah and provide a way for Jerusalem to be rebuilt and fortified.

4. Nehemiah Addressed Him as "Great and Awesome" (v. 5).
In addition to the three names Nehemiah used, he also described God with two adjectives that carry a great deal of meaning: "great" and "awesome."

The word "great" in Hebrew is *gadowl*, and it emphasizes God's superlative significance and immeasurable value. There is none superior to our living Lord; He has the wisdom and ability to do anything He wishes. And because of His amazing love for us, we know He always has our very best interests at heart.

> *Although Nehemiah was merely a servant in the eyes of Artaxerxes, he served the God who governed the ruler.*

Isaiah tells us, "Because of the greatness of His might and the strength of His power, not one of them [the vast host of stars] is missing" (Isa. 40:26). This alone should cause us to praise and magnify His name. Likewise, King David wrote,

> Great is the LORD, and highly to be praised,
> And His greatness is unsearchable.
> One generation shall praise Your works to another,
> And shall declare Your mighty acts.
> On the glorious splendor of Your majesty
> And on Your wonderful works, I will meditate.
> Men shall speak of the power of Your awesome acts,

And I will tell of Your greatness.
They shall eagerly utter the memory of
   Your abundant goodness
And will shout joyfully of
   Your righteousness. (Ps. 145:3–7)

Understanding the Lord's greatness should help us recognize our proper positions before Him as it did Nehemiah.

This leads us to the second adjective, "awesome," which comes from the Hebrew term *yare*. People usually use "awesome" to describe things that are great in size or especially wonderful. The Hebrew meaning is somewhat deeper and more significant. You see, the verb *yare* means "to fear." Instead of "awesome," some translations use "terrible" or "terrifying" to convey how worthy the Holy God is of our utmost reverence and respect.

That does not mean you and I should be frightened of the Lord. As believers, we have no reason to be scared away from our loving heavenly Father (1 Thess. 5:9). In fact, 1 John 4:18 admonishes, "There is no fear in love; but perfect love casts out fear, because fear involves punishment, and the one who fears is not perfected in love."

Instead, God's awesome character should inspire us to take all He says very seriously. After all, He is holy, righteous, and just—the only One worthy of our highest respect, praise, and worship.

A Humble Progression

Nehemiah deeply understood the greatness and holiness of the Lord. So when he prayed, he did not take being in God's presence lightly. After all, Nehemiah was addressing the One True God:

- *YHWH*—the eternally existing Life Giver
- *Elohim*—the mighty and faithful Covenant Keeper
- *Adonai*—the Sovereign Lord and Provider of all that exists
- *The great and awesome God*—who is above all, absolutely holy, and worthy of our reverence

It is most likely that Solomon had a similar understanding of the Lord when he wrote, "Guard your steps as you go to the house of God and draw near to listen rather than to offer the sacrifice of fools; for they do not know they are doing evil. Do not be hasty in word or impulsive in thought to bring up a matter in the presence of God. For God is in heaven and you are on the earth; therefore let your words be few" (Eccl. 5:1–2).

> *The counsel of heaven should be received and obeyed with the utmost respect.*

With all his great knowledge, Solomon realized that the Lord was still much wiser than he could ever be. The counsel of heaven should be received and obeyed with the utmost respect.

So when we come to Nehemiah's conversation with God, we know he was sincerely, seriously, and humbly seeking the Lord's guidance. He prayed:

"I beseech You, O LORD God of heaven, the great and awesome God, who preserves the covenant and loving kindness for those who love Him and keep His commandments, let Your ear now be attentive and Your eyes open to hear the prayer of Your servant which I am praying before You now, day and night, on behalf of the sons of Israel Your servants, confessing the sins of the sons of Israel which we have sinned against You; I and my father's house have sinned. We have acted very corruptly against You and have not kept the commandments, nor the statutes, nor the ordinances which You commanded Your servant Moses. Remember the word which You commanded Your servant Moses, saying, 'If you are unfaithful I will scatter you among the peoples; but if you return to Me and keep My commandments and do them, though those of you who have been scattered were in the most remote part of the heavens, I will gather them from there and will bring them to the place where I have chosen to cause My name to dwell.' They are Your servants and Your people whom You redeemed by Your great power and by Your strong hand. O Lord, I beseech You, may Your ear be attentive to the prayer of Your servant and the prayer of Your servants who delight to revere Your name, and make Your servant successful today and grant him compassion before this man." (Neh. 1:5–11)

Perhaps you have noticed that Nehemiah's attention was on the Lord and rightly relating to Him, instead of the problem that drove him to pray—the broken walls and burnt gates of Jerusalem. It is dangerous for us to allow our difficulties to reside in the forefront of our thinking. Rather, our focus should always remain on our matchless God, who can triumph over any trouble we bring to Him.

> *Our focus should always remain on our matchless God, who can triumph over any trouble we bring to Him.*

Therefore, realizing Nehemiah's exalted view of the Lord, let us note the progression of his godly prayer.

First, Nehemiah Praised God (v. 5).
This is understandable but also important and instructive. Nehemiah begins with an accurate view of the Lord and what He is able to accomplish. He fully believed that God *could* and *would* preserve the covenant He had made with His people, and save them from their distresses. We must approach the Father with the same attitude. We must know who He is and express our trust in His matchless character and ability.

Second, Nehemiah Exhibited Faith That the
Lord Would Respond to His Prayer (v. 6).

No matter how hopeless the situation seemed or how unable he felt to solve the problem, Nehemiah understood the power of calling on the Father. He didn't know how or when God would answer, but he trusted that He would. Do we approach the Lord with the same confidence and anticipation?

Third, Nehemiah Confessed His Sins (vv. 6–8).

Nehemiah understood that the people of Judah were in this situation as a consequence of their sinfulness. He did not blame God for abandoning them or question the Lord's goodness. Rather, Nehemiah acknowledged the fault of the people in disobeying Him, thereby identifying the problem that was hindering their progress. We would do well to do the same, because if we want to see the power of God, we must first seek to be pure at heart (Ps. 66:16–18).

Fourth, Nehemiah Recalled God's Promises (vv. 9–10).

Nehemiah remembered the Lord's pledge in Deuteronomy 30:2–3, "Return to the Lord your God and obey Him with all your heart and soul . . . then the Lord your God will restore you from captivity, and have compassion on you, and will gather you again from all the peoples where the Lord your God has scattered you." This undoubtedly gave Nehemiah great comfort in his time of need. Because the Father always keeps His word, we can be confident that He will honor His promises to us.

Fifth, Nehemiah Expressed His Willingness to Be Used for God's Purposes (v. 11).

This godly man understood that he was in a unique position to help the people of Judah because of his proximity to King Artaxerxes. Yet he also realized that if he displeased Artaxerxes when he addressed him about reversing his own decree (Ezra 4:17–23), the king could have him executed. Of course, he would obey the Lord's will regardless of the risks, since he truly believed God was in control. He prayed, "Make Your servant successful today and grant him compassion before this man" (Neh. 1:11). Likewise, God may call us to do things that appear difficult or unreasonable, but He still wants us to obey. Do we truly believe He is able to help us?

> *God may call us to do things that appear difficult or unreasonable, but He still wants us to obey.*

THE REAL PURPOSE

The temptation at this point is to jump in and talk about all the miraculous things God did through Nehemiah, and we will do so in the next chapter. However, that would focus our attention on what the Lord *did* rather than *who He is*. How He responds to our prayers is significant, to be sure, and we will cover that. But how you and I relate to Him is even more important.

You see, *your intimacy with God—His first priority for your life—determines the impact of your life.* If you do not have an adequate view of who He is, you will find yourself doubting and wavering during your most crucial moments. This is because you respond to God in proportion to what you believe about Him.

Consider: If you had been in Nehemiah's position, how would you have prayed? Would you have been confident in the Father's character and His willingness to act on your behalf? Would you have called Him *YHWH, Elohim,* or *Adonai* in full faith and trust?

There are many other names of God throughout Scripture; perhaps they resonate with you. The following is only a partial list, but think about each one. Circle those that mean the most to you:

- Almighty God (Gen. 17:1–2, *El Shaddai*)
- Faithful and True (Rev. 19:11)
- Father to the fatherless (Ps. 68:5)
- King of Glory (Ps. 24:8)
- King of kings and Lord of lords (1 Tim. 6:15–16)
- Our Great High Priest (Heb. 4:14–16)
- Savior of the World (1 John 4:14–15)
- The Everlasting God (Isa. 40:28–31, *El Olam*)
- The God who sees me (Gen. 16:13, *El Roi*)
- The Great Physician (Mark 2:17)
- The Lord our Banner (Ex. 17:8–15, *Jehovah Nissi*)

- The Lord our Great Provider (Gen. 22:9–14, *Jehovah Jireh*)
- The Lord our Healer (Ex. 15:26, *Jehovah Rapha*)
- The Lord our Deliverer (Ps. 70:4–5)
- The Lord our Peace (Judg. 6:11–24, *Jehovah Shalom*)
- The Lord our Redeemer (Isa. 48:17, *Haggo'el*)
- The Lord our Refuge and Fortress (Ps. 91:2–4)
- The Lord our Righteousness (Jer. 23:5–6, *Jehovah Tsidkenu*)
- The Lord our Rock (2 Sam. 22:47, *Jehovah Tsuri*)
- The Lord our Sanctifier (Ex. 31:13, *Jehovah Mekaddishkem*)
- The Lord our Shepherd (Ps. 23, *Jehovah Rohi*)
- Wonderful Counselor (Isa. 9.6)

Some of these names may mean a great deal to you; others you may desire to comprehend better. You might not fully grasp how the Lord can be your refuge and fortress during times of difficulty, though you long to feel safe in His care. Or maybe you want to be free of some sin in your life and wish to know Him as your Deliverer. We all have areas in our lives where we must grow in our understanding of who He is.

> *We all have areas in our lives where we must grow in our understanding of who He is.*

There was a time in my own life when

I wrestled with knowing the Father more deeply. Although the church was growing well and everything else in my life seemed fantastic, I struggled inwardly. I could not identify what the encumbrance was, no matter how much I sought the Lord and prayed. I called my four closest friends, who were all godly men, and said, "God is trying to teach me something, but I don't know what it is, and I need your help to figure it out. Here's what I want to do: I will tell you everything that I know about myself—good, bad, and indifferent. Then I would like the four of you to confer about what I should do. Whatever you agree to tell me, I'll do it. I know you're all listening to God."

We started about two o'clock in the afternoon and talked until ten o'clock that first night. After they went to bed, I wrote out seventeen legal-sized pages of experiences from my life I didn't want to forget to tell them.

The next day, we conversed for several more hours. Finally, one of the men said, "Charles, put your head on the table and close your eyes." I did. Quietly, he asked me, "Imagine your father just picked you up in his arms and held you. What do you feel?" He knew that my father had died when I was nine months old, and that his loss had a tremendous impact on my life.

Immediately, I burst out crying, and I continued weeping for a long time. Still, I did not understand what was causing so much emotion. He asked me again, "What do you feel, Charles?"

The feelings were so overpowering, it was a long time before I could answer him. At last I replied, "I felt hugged, like I was warm and secure. I felt . . . loved." I realized that until that day, I had never really experienced God's love. I had told others about His love but had never truly sensed it myself.

That day changed my life. The time with my four friends transformed my ministry and everything I felt about the Christian life; the Father's love had become real to me and extremely powerful.

I challenge you to do the same. Put your head down and imagine the Father holding you. You may be surprised by the emotions you feel. You may, as I did, realize His overwhelming love for you. It is possible that you feel like squirming in His arms and pushing Him away because, somewhere in your heart, you do not trust Him. A sense of conviction may come over you due to some unconfessed sin. You may realize that you've been running away from Him all of your life when all you've wanted to do is feel safe in your heavenly Father's arms.

Whatever the case, be still and allow God to deal with whatever emotions and issues arise. Do not fear. He will teach you what to do.

The Father can remove any encumbrance you have to knowing Him, and He can draw you into a deeper, more intimate relationship than you have ever known. Trust Him.

As I said at the beginning of this chapter, what makes prayer the ultimate conversation is not necessarily the subject matter or the circumstances surrounding the dialogue but with whom you are speaking. It is of utmost importance for you to settle in your heart who you believe God is.

Now I am going to ask you to answer the following questions. Be completely honest. This is between you and the Father, so ask Him to search your heart and reveal the truth about what you think. Remember, there are no wrong answers, just a continually growing relationship with Him.

Ask yourself:

- Do I truly trust God?
- Am I confident that the Lord has the ability to help me?
- Am I convinced that the Father is willing to listen to me and come to my aid?

I hope you are. But if your answer to any of these questions is no, I pray that God will do a mighty work in your life and show you beyond a shadow of a doubt that you can place all your hope in Him. Not only is He worthy of your trust, but He also loves you unconditionally and wants to show you life at its very best.

Allow Him to reveal Himself to you.

Father, how grateful we are for Your loving-kindness in allowing us to know You personally and to pray to You. We know what a wonderful privilege it is to have the ultimate conversation with You, so we honor You as the Great I Am,

YHWH, Elohim, *and* Adonai. *We praise You, Sovereign Lord of heaven and earth, the great and awesome God who unfailingly keeps all of Your promises to those who love and obey You.*

Father, we thank You for hearing the prayers of Your servants today. Lord, if there are any unconfessed sins in our lives, please call them to mind so that we can repent of them immediately. We want to be faithful and glorify You with our lives. We are exceedingly grateful that the matchless name of Jesus cleanses us from all of our unrighteousness.

Father, we recall the promise You made to us through the prophet Jeremiah today: "You will seek Me and find Me when you search for Me with all your heart" (29:13). I pray that as this reader seeks to know You better, You will remove all of the encumbrances that remain in this dear soul's life. May this individual truly understand who You are and enjoy time in Your presence fully.

Lord, may Your ear be attentive to the prayer of Your servant and all those who delight to revere Your name. May we honor and glorify You today and every day.

In Jesus' holy and wonderful name, I pray. Amen.

3

THE GOD WHO ANSWERS

He Is Faithful to Show You His Will

GOD CARES ENOUGH ABOUT US to reveal Himself to us. The Father formed humankind in His image for the specific purpose of fellowshipping with and relating to us deeply. From the beginning of creation, we see the Lord speaking to those He created (Gen. 1; John 1:1). His first interaction with Adam in the Garden of Eden was to bless him, give the man purpose, and initiate a relationship with him. Psalm 14:2 tells us that since then, "The LORD has looked down from heaven upon the sons of men to see if there are any who understand, who seek after God."

In the previous chapter, we discussed how important it is for us to have an accurate view of the Father and *expect* Him to answer us. But you and I cannot have a relationship with someone who doesn't communicate with us in a way we can grasp. Some reading this may doubt that God talks to anyone anymore. They face trials and difficulties and ask, "Lord, where are You in the midst of all this?" They have never heard His voice and wonder if they ever will.

I can assure you, the Lord is speaking to you and me today. God is an awesome communicator who is always drawing us into conversation with Him (John 6:44; 12:32). We can count on the fact that God wants to have a conversation with us and that He begins speaking with us long before we ever ask Him for anything.

However, let me make something clear: The Lord doesn't usually address us in such a radical way as He did Moses—speaking to him from a burning bush (Ex. 3)—although we may wish He would. Nor will His glorious presence always be so overpowering that we fall on our faces like the people of Israel, Ezekiel, and Saul did (Lev. 9:23–24; Ezek. 3:22–23; Acts 9:1–9). At times, God's voice comes to us as a quiet whisper (1 Kings 19:11–13) or an internal prompting of the Holy Spirit (Luke 2:27–28).

> *God is an awesome communicator who is always drawing us into conversation with Him.*

How the Father communicates is not as important as the fact that He wants to connect with you. If you are walking with Him daily and obeying Him, you *will* see His supernatural intervention in your life and hear His voice gently instructing your heart. I guarantee it.

BACK TO NEHEMIAH

As an example, let us look at how the Lord responded to Nehemiah. When we last discussed Nehemiah, he was facing a terrible challenge.

Israel's enemies, Rehum and Shimshai, had convinced the Persian king Artaxerxes to stop any rebuilding of Jerusalem's walls (Ezra 4:8–23). They said:

> Let it be known to the king that the Jews who came up from you have come to us at Jerusalem; they are rebuilding the rebellious and evil city and are finishing the walls and repairing the foundations. Now let it be known to the king, that if that city is rebuilt and the walls are finished, they will not pay tribute, custom or toll. . . . And you will discover in the record books and learn that that city is a rebellious city and damaging to kings and provinces, and that they have incited revolt within it in past days. (Ezra 4:13, 15)

Believing that the Jews were planning to rebel against Persia, Artaxerxes decreed, "Make these men stop *work,* that this city may not be rebuilt until a decree is issued by me" (Ezra 4:21). Because of this decree, the people of Jerusalem remained unprotected and in continual danger.

By the time Nehemiah received word of the city's condition, the gates had been burned and the portion of wall that had been reconstructed had been torn down again. The Jews there were constantly oppressed and mistreated.

As cupbearer to the king, Nehemiah realized he was in a unique position to help his people because of his proximity to Artaxerxes. Yet he also understood he could be executed if the king perceived his request to resume construction on Jerusalem's walls as treacherous or rebellious.

Regardless of the consequences, Nehemiah submitted himself to the Lord in prayer, acknowledging Him as *YHWH, Elohim, Adonai,* and the great and awesome God. Whatever the Father asked him to do, he would obey.

GOD'S RESPONSE TO NEHEMIAH'S PRAYER

One might think that after such a reverent, courageously obedient, and beautiful prayer (Neh. 1:5–11), the Lord would respond to Nehemiah immediately and with great fanfare. I'm sure Nehemiah would have preferred a quick, unmistakably supernatural reply. However, just as you and I must sometimes wait on God's answers, so did this godly cupbearer.

Nehemiah 1:1 tells us that he began praying for Jerusalem in the Jewish month of Chislev, which occurs during our November and December. But in Nehemiah 2:1, we find that the Lord didn't provide Nehemiah with an opportunity to address the king until Nisan, which is equivalent to our March and April. This means Nehemiah waited roughly three to four months before seeing the Father's movement in regard to his petitions.

Was God silent during this time? Absolutely not. The Lord

was actively preparing Nehemiah for the task ahead, whether he realized it or not. It was the Father who gave Nehemiah the burden for the people of Jerusalem in the first place—even before he began to pray.

This is why you and I should never lose heart or take matters into our own hands if the Lord seems to tarry in responding to some request. As we see in the story of Nehemiah, God has His own timing and works on behalf of those who wait for Him (Isa. 64:4). When His plans began to

God has His own timing and works on behalf of those who wait for Him.

be revealed, it was breathtaking to see how powerfully He had provided for Nehemiah and the needs of Jerusalem.

1. Favor with King Artaxerxes

First, God opened Artaxerxes' eyes to see that something was amiss with his cupbearer. Nehemiah reports, "The king said to me, 'Why is your face sad though you are not sick? This is nothing but sadness of heart.' Then I was very much afraid" (Neh. 2:2). Nehemiah did not intend for his sorrow to show. As a servant, he was required to appear cheerful before the king. However, Artaxerxes took note that something was wrong, and suddenly, Nehemiah had an open door of opportunity to state his case. This was the moment. This was what he had asked the Lord to provide.

Nehemiah responded boldly, "Let the king live forever. Why should my face not be sad when the city, the place of my fathers' tombs, lies desolate and its gates have been consumed by fire?" (Neh. 2:3). Though it was a bold statement, it intrigued Artaxerxes, and he asked Nehemiah what was needed to fix the problem.

It is doubtful that many kings in history have asked their cupbearer, "What can I do to help you?" Yet there is no limit to what the Father can do to help His beloved people. In verse 5, Nehemiah tells us, "I prayed to the God of heaven." It must have been one of the shortest spontaneous petitions in history, but it was immensely important. You see, Nehemiah was inviting Elohim into his interaction with the king—undoubtedly asking the Lord of lords to guide the conversation and give him success.

Nehemiah was inviting Elohim into his interaction with the king— undoubtedly asking the Lord of lords to guide the conversation and give him success.

At the end of the encounter, Nehemiah was able to report, "The king granted them [the requests] to me because the good hand of my God was on me" (Neh. 2:8). Artaxerxes gave him permission to leave, a military escort, and the letters he needed for safe passage and timber. Best of all, the king reversed his decree and allowed the people to recommence building the walls of Jerusalem.

2. Authority in Jerusalem

The second challenge Nehemiah faced was that he was a stranger in Jerusalem and had no reason to be accepted as a leader. Also, he was no engineer, expert in construction, or even military commander; he was merely a cupbearer to the Persian king. What right did he have to ask the people to follow him? No one had been able to fully rebuild the walls in the 140 years since the Babylonians destroyed them. Did Nehemiah really think he could motivate the Jews to rise up against all the opposition and succeed in this overwhelming task?

Nehemiah understood his precarious position going into Jerusalem. He wrote, "I did not tell anyone what my God was putting into my mind to do for Jerusalem" (Neh. 2:12). Instead, he quietly surveyed the situation, trusting that the Father would give him the right plan and words at the appropriate time. And that is exactly what happened.

It was not the cleverness of Nehemiah's message but the Spirit of the living Lord in it that gave it power.

Nehemiah told the priests, nobles, and officials of Jerusalem: "You see the bad situation we are in, that Jerusalem is desolate and its gates burned by fire. Come, let us rebuild the wall of Jerusalem so that we will no longer be a reproach" (Neh. 2:17). He also testified about what God had already done through Artaxerxes to provide building materials for the city.

It was not the cleverness of Nehemiah's message but the Spirit of the living Lord in it that gave it power. Nehemiah did not have to give an elaborate discourse or motivational speech. He didn't have to campaign or convince anyone to let him lead. No, Nehemiah simply told the people of Jerusalem what the Father was calling them to accomplish, and they immediately responded to God's invitation.

"Let us arise and build" (Neh. 2:18), they said, and construction started. Only the Father could have moved their hearts to bring about such agreement—even enthusiasm—for such a daunting endeavor that had failed so many times.

3. Protection from Attacks

Although Nehemiah had overwhelming support from the Jewish community in Jerusalem, from the very beginning of his time there, he faced opposition from enemies who preferred an unfortified and vulnerable Israel (Neh. 2:10).

Sanballat, the governor of Samaria, criticized the efforts: "What are these feeble Jews doing? Are they going to restore it for themselves? . . . Can they revive the stones from the dusty rubble even the burned ones?" (Neh. 4:2). No doubt the builders were asking some of these questions themselves. After all, the Jews were a poor and oppressed people who had seen previous efforts defeated by outside attacks. And Sanballat had a point: In certain places, the stone for building was cracked and charred.

Others joined in the ridicule, such as Tobiah, who was a

ruler in Ammon. He said, "Even what they are building—
if a fox should jump on *it,* he would break their stone wall
down!" In other words, their work was so flimsy that even a
small creature could knock it over with barely any effort.

Their words discouraged the builders. Thankfully, God
answered Nehemiah's prayers and strengthened the Jews. And
"the people worked with all their heart" (Neh. 4:6 NIV).

Unfortunately, their enemies were not deterred. Seeing
that their mockery was not sufficient to dissuade the people
from building, Sanballat, Tobiah, and others "conspired together to come *and* fight against Jerusalem and to cause a dis-
turbance in it" (Neh. 4:8). The pressure increased, as did the
warnings about plots to destroy the newly constructed wall.
The Jews grew more weary and frightened.

Have you ever been in a situation like this? Your difficulties begin with others' criticism, and before you know it, your
opponents escalate to real and piercing intimidation, threat-
ening the people and things you love most. The anxiety can
become so paralyzing that you actually consider retreat.

From a human perspective, the Jews were understand-
ably fearful concerning their homes and families. However,
Nehemiah understood that those enemies had no power to
thwart the plans of the living God. As he had done before,
he turned to the Father in prayer and encouraged the people,
"Do not be afraid of them; remember the Lord who is great
and awesome. . . . Our God will fight for us" (Neh. 4:14, 20).

We saw in the last chapter that the words "great" and
"awesome" signify there is no one superior to God: He has

the wisdom and ability to do anything He pleases. Nehemiah was reminding people that there was only One they should fear—only One worthy of their reverence, respect, and obedience. He was the One who would defend them without fail. As King David once declared, "In God I have put my trust; I shall not be afraid. What can mere man do to me?" (Ps. 56:4).

> *There is only One we should fear—only One worthy of our reverence, respect, and obedience. He is the One who will defend.*

Again, the Lord answered them by honoring their faith and showing the Jews how to protect themselves from attack. Nehemiah reported, "Our enemies learned that we knew of their plot, and that God had exposed and frustrated their plan" (Neh. 4:15 TLB).

4. *Guidance to Victory*

Although there were other crises along the way, the Father continued to be Jerusalem's shield and defense. Much to the surprise of their enemies, the Jews rebuilt the wall in just *fifty-two days* (Neh. 6:15). It was a miracle. The fortifications that had lain in ruins for 140 years were successfully reconstructed *in less than two months*—a victory that would not have been possible if the Lord had not been actively speaking into the situation.

Even Israel's adversaries acknowledged that God had accomplished this great thing on their behalf. Nehemiah wrote:

"When all our enemies heard *of it*, and all the nations surrounding us saw *it*, they lost their confidence; for they recognized that this work had been accomplished with the help of
our God" (Neh. 6:16).

Because Nehemiah heard the Father
and faithfully responded to His call, more
people began listening to Him. Spiritual
revival came powerfully to Jerusalem
(Neh. 8).

There was no burning-bush experience or other great sign from the Lord
about how Nehemiah was to proceed. But
every day that the cupbearer spent time in
the Father's presence, God was speaking
to his heart and teaching him what to do.
And because he was listening, he had an
enormous influence on other people's lives
and on the future of an entire nation.

*The fortifications
that had lain
in ruins for
140 years were
successfully
reconstructed in
less than two
months—a
victory that would
not have been
possible without
the Lord.*

GOD IS SPEAKING TO YOU

Nehemiah's story shows us that you and I have the greatest
effect when we have an ongoing conversation with the Father
and humbly submit to His direction.

The Lord may call us, as He did Nehemiah, to tasks that
seem daunting and impossible. Those assignments tend to appear more difficult because of our human inadequacies—we

imagine that all circumstances are against us, and we feel weak and powerless to complete God's missions.

It may be that we face some of the same obstacles Nehemiah did: We have people in authority over us who are preventing our progress; we do not have the influence or resources necessary to proceed; or the criticisms of others have wounded us deeply and have paralyzed us from going forward. We may even face spiritual warfare—the enemy has taken aim at those places in our lives that are already painful and cause us to question everything we believe about God and what He has called us to accomplish. If we are not careful, discouragement can set in, leaving us afraid, depressed, confused, and questioning the Father.

> *If the Lord calls us to a task, He will help us accomplish it, regardless of what anyone thinks or says.*

What we must remember in such circumstances is that *only the truth matters* and the struggles we're facing represent a *faith battle.* Will we listen to the threats of men or trust the promises of God? Will we allow our circumstances to dishearten us or believe in His unfailing character? Either we will believe the Father takes full responsibility for our needs when we obey Him—including our safety—or we won't.

Let me be clear: If the Lord calls us to a task, He *will* help us accomplish it, regardless of what anyone thinks or says.

The Lord Will *Reveal His Plan*

You may be thinking, *This is all well and good, but I need God's answer* now. *I don't know what He wants me to do. Will He really talk to me?*

Let me assure you, if you are seeking God and are prepared to obey Him, He will move heaven and earth to show you His will. Jesus promised, "Ask, and it will be given to you; seek, and you will find; knock, and it will be opened to you. For everyone who asks receives, and he who seeks finds, and to him who knocks it will be opened" (Matt. 7:7–8). I can assure you, the Savior has never failed in keeping this promise.

Again, however, He does not always answer us immediately. I recall a particularly difficult season during my senior year at the University of Richmond. Everything seemed to be going wrong, and I was completely miserable. It was exam week, and I had received a fifty on one test and a seventy-five on another. This was terrible, because I was a senior, and it seemed as if I'd spent all this time in school just to fail. I was desperate to know God's plan and purpose for my life, but I felt as if He had completely walked out on me—as if He were gone.

At one point, the pressure grew so great and my struggle so intense, I went to see my prayer partners. On my way, I said, "Father, I've got to be absolutely sure what Your will is for me. I've prayed, asked, pleaded, begged, and fasted. I've done everything I know to do. God, please do *something*—my whole future is based on You. Please clarify this question in my mind and show me exactly what to do." I am sure you can relate to the pressure I was under.

Then the Lord brought to mind something my grandfather George Washington Stanley had told me. He had gone through a similar time in his life when he was confused and seeking God's guidance about whether to preach. My grandfather didn't have an education and could barely read or write. He was feeling inadequate and doubtful about his future. Granddad said he got down on his knees and asked the Father to show him what to do. Then he got specific. He said, "Lord, if You are calling me to preach the gospel, let me see two falling stars." Sure enough, he looked up and saw two bright lights streaming across the night sky.

I thought, *If Granddad asked God for something that specific and the Lord answered, then maybe He will do the same for me.* After all, my grandfather never doubted that the Father had called him to preach. And the Lord used him in a wonderful way; he planted numerous churches and led many people to Jesus.

So I prayed, *God, I know I don't have any business asking You this, but if this is Your will for my life—if this is really what You're calling me to do—please let me see two falling stars like my grandfather did.* A couple of evenings later, I looked up and saw two brilliant meteors shooting across the night sky at the same time. It was as if the Lord said to me, "You asked Me, and I've answered your prayer." I fell on my face and thanked Him with all my heart.

If the Father had not spoken to me in such a powerful way, I may have given up, and the course of my life would have been altered completely. But I can say for certain that not once since then have I ever doubted His call.

Why Can We Trust the Father to Reveal His Will?

Likewise, the Lord is speaking to *you*. The Father is drawing you into a conversation, speaking to you about His plans for your life, revealing Himself to you, and confirming what He would like to do in and through you.

Perhaps you are in a place like I was. You are desperate to hear God, because some trial, temptation, or challenge is tearing you asunder. Don't give up. Even if you have been pursuing His direction for a while, keep seeking, asking, and knocking.

In His love for us, God has made it possible for us to know without a shadow of a doubt what His plans for us are in any given situation. Moreover, we can be certain that the Father will move heaven and earth to show us His will. However, what He intends to tell us may be so crucial that He wants to make sure we are fully focused on Him. So any waiting we experience is simply intended to fix our attention on Him and prepare us for His answer.

> *We can be certain that the Father will move heaven and earth to show us His will.*

Why can we be sure? Because He says in Jeremiah 29:11, " 'I know the plans that I have for you,' declares the LORD, 'plans for welfare and not for calamity to give you a future and a hope.'" This is His assurance. Think about it: How can God expect us to walk in His will and accomplish His purposes if He doesn't tell us what they are? It would be out of the Father's character to hide what He wants us to be and do.

When we look at the promises in Scripture, it becomes clear that the Lord is not merely disposed to showing us what to do but actively seeking to reveal to us His path of life:

- "In Your loving-kindness You have led the people whom You have redeemed." (Ex. 15:13)
- "You will make known to me the path of life; in Your presence is fullness of joy." (Ps. 16:11)
- "He guides me in the paths of righteousness for His name's sake." (Ps. 23:3)
- "Who is the man who fears the LORD? He will instruct him in the way he should choose." (Ps. 25:12)
- "He led forth His own people like sheep and guided them in the wilderness like a flock; He led them safely, so that they did not fear." (Ps. 78:52–53)
- "Teach me to do Your will, for You are my God; let Your good Spirit lead me on level ground." (Ps. 143:10)
- "Trust in the LORD with all your heart and do not lean on your own understanding. In all your ways

acknowledge Him, and He will make your paths straight." (Prov. 3:5–6)

- "I have directed you in the way of wisdom; I have led you in upright paths." (Prov. 4:11)
- "Your Teacher will no longer hide Himself, but your eyes will behold your Teacher. Your ears will hear a word behind you, 'This is the way, walk in it,' whenever you turn to the right or to the left." (Isa. 30:20–21)
- "I will lead the blind by a way they do not know, in paths they do not know I will guide them. I will make darkness into light before them and rugged places into plains." (Isa. 42:16)
- "Thus says the LORD, your Redeemer, the Holy One of Israel, 'I am the LORD your God, who teaches you to profit, who leads you in the way you should go.' " (Isa. 48:17)
- "All who are being led by the Spirit of God, these are sons of God." (Rom. 8:14)
- "We have not ceased to pray for you and to ask that you may be filled with the knowledge of His will in all spiritual wisdom and understanding." (Col. 1:9)

In those moments when you are desperate to hear God's voice and His answer to your inquiries, remember His promises and count on them. Continue watching for His activity and listening for His voice. He is getting your attention and will assuredly show you His will.

YOUR GOOD SHEPHERD SPEAKS

Remember, Jesus said, "I am the good shepherd; and I know My sheep, and am known by My own. . . . I lay down My life for the sheep. . . . My sheep hear My voice, and I know them, and they follow Me. And I give them eternal life, and they shall never perish; neither shall anyone snatch them out of My hand" (John 10:14–15, 27–28).

In biblical times, shepherds dedicated their lives to the well-being of their flocks and were connected to their sheep, even to the point of giving each one a name. It was their responsibility to put themselves between their flocks and danger. They tenderly cared for all their needs.

This is the image that Jesus uses to describe His relationship with us—our Good Shepherd is always there to guide, protect, and care for each of us. The Lord speaks for our good, desiring to give us what is best and to protect us from harm.

Therefore, as your Shepherd, God communicates with you in many ways:

He Speaks with You Personally

In the beloved 23rd Psalm, King David wrote: "The LORD is *my* shepherd" (23:1, emphasis added). The Father knows exactly what is happening to you at this very moment. Likewise, He understands where you have been and where you're going. As you read this, you may wonder whether He grasps the pressure you're under and the immense need you have for His direction, comfort, healing, and wisdom. Yes, He does. Every detail of your life is in His sovereign care (Matt. 10:29–31). Stop worrying and begin trusting Him. The God who governs the affairs of the world cares for you *intimately* and *individually*. He will not fail you.

> *Every detail of your life is in His sovereign care. Stop worrying and begin trusting Him.*

He Speaks with You About His Wise Provision

David continued by writing, "The LORD is my shepherd, *I shall not want*" (Ps. 23:1, emphasis added). Perhaps you have lacked many things and have a hard time believing this promise. But the Good Shepherd wants you to have what is best, so He will always give you what you truly need (Phil. 4:19). He supplies not only what you physically require but also your emotional and spiritual needs—satisfying your soul with love, acceptance, companionship, and worth as no one else can.

Also, you can always trust what the Father tells you because He will never lead you to anything that could harm you (Matt. 7:9–11). Even when He prevents you from receiving something you desire and you don't understand His purposes, you can have complete confidence that He has a good reason for how He guides and directs your life (Isa. 30:18, 64:4; James 1:2–6). It has been my experience that when God said no to one blessing, it was so I could experience a greater one later on. The same is true for you.

He Speaks with Mercy and Grace

I am keenly aware that some are almost afraid to listen to the Lord because of the guilt and shame they feel in their lives. They fear that if they open their ears to His voice, all they'll hear is condemnation and wrath, confirming their feelings of worthlessness. Yet David's testimony about the Shepherd speaks of His loving grace—which builds up rather than tearing down. David writes, "He restores my soul; He guides me in the paths of righteousness for His name's sake" (Ps. 23:3). In other words, when we submit to Him as a sheep to its shepherd, the Father brings healing, wholeness, and a restored understanding of our purpose.

> *It has been my experience that when God said no to one blessing, it was so I could experience a greater one later on.*

The reason God hates sin is because it creates emptiness, guilt, anger, and loneliness within your heart and separates you from Him. So He heals you of your transgressions through the death and resurrection of His Son Jesus Christ (Acts 2:38; 1 John 1:9), and He gives you the Holy Spirit to teach you to walk in a manner worthy of His child (John 14:26).

The Good Shepherd understands that every one of us will stray at some point (Isa. 53:6). But He calls you back to the throne of grace to show you mercy, to restore your soul, and to remind you of your overwhelming worth in His sight—never to make you feel worse.

He Speaks Through His Protection

I cannot remember when I did not have a paper route growing up. I delivered newspapers twice a day until I went away to college, and it was through this occupation that I learned that God was my Shield and Deliverer just like the psalmist said: "The LORD is my rock and my fortress and my deliverer, my God, my rock, in whom I take refuge; my shield and the horn of my salvation" (Ps. 18:2).

As we confess our sins and seek His forgiveness, the Father brings healing, wholeness, and a restored understanding of our purpose.

Like any paperboy, I had my share of mean dogs and customers who refused to pay. I quoted Scripture at the dogs and prayed for the stingy customers. It was on the afternoon route, however, that I needed the Lord to be my Deliverer and Shield.

This was because North Main Street in Danville, Virginia, was a major thoroughfare and I had to cross it several times a day, which meant my life was in constant danger. One day I was stepping out into the street when a speeding car screeched to a halt inches away from me.

A woman whose paper I had delivered for several years yelled from her porch, "Charles Stanley, don't you dare get killed in front of my house!" I replied, "Yes, ma'am," as if it were up to me. But I knew it was God who had protected me from that car, and He had a plan for my life. Because of that, I was not afraid to get back up and finish my route. I knew my life was in the Good Shepherd's hands.

Everyone experiences trials, dangers, heartaches, and doubts. We all face situations where we feel vulnerable, abandoned, and helpless. We wonder why the Lord would allow us to experience such hazards, pain, and suffering if He truly cares about us. The questions run rampant in our minds: *Has He forsaken me? Why can't I hear His voice? Why doesn't He deliver me? Doesn't He care about me?* The truth of the matter is, we often learn to listen to God more closely and depend upon Him more fully as we walk with Him through adversity.

David gives us this powerful testimony: "Even though I walk through the valley of the shadow of death, I fear no evil, for You are with me; Your rod and Your staff, they comfort me" (Ps. 23:4). He learned that the Father's presence with him was an undeniable *fact,* and we can, too.

As believers, we're promised that no matter how hopeless or perilous our circumstances may appear, the Lord will never leave us; He will faithfully lead us through every difficulty (Deut. 31:8). We are also assured that He will transform all of our trials into something positive in our lives (Isa. 30:20–21; Rom. 8:28). Because our Good Shepherd protects us, we know that our troubles will not leave lasting scars. Instead, each obstacle we face builds our characters and brings us closer to Him than we've ever been (1 Pet. 1:6–9).

He Speaks to Prepare Us

Finally, a great deal of what the Father communicates is to ready us for eternity. Remember, in John 17:3, Jesus tells us, "This is eternal life, that they may know You, the only true God, and Jesus Christ whom You have sent." The Lord's first and foremost goal is to bring you deeper into an intimate relationship with Him.

David writes, "You have anointed my head with oil; my cup overflows. Surely goodness and loving-kindness will follow me all the days of my life, and I will dwell in the house of the Lord forever" (Ps. 23:5–6). What a wonderful promise! It is an assurance that the Father wants you to take hold of, regardless of your circumstances: His goodness and loving-kindness will be with you forever—even into eternity (John 14:2–3).

We often learn to listen to God more closely and depend upon Him more fully as we walk with Him through adversity.

You may not know what the future holds for you, but God does (Isa. 46:10). Your Good Shepherd understands the path ahead better than you ever could, and He is actively preparing you for it. He has gone before you to map out the best route to get you where you need to be. And He will always be sure you have everything you need to succeed.

YOUR GOOD SHEPHERD SPEAKS—
ARE YOU LISTENING?

The Lord cares enough about us to reveal Himself to us. Your God, the Good Shepherd, speaks. He communicates with you personally about His wise provision, with mercy and grace, through His protection, and to prepare you for all that is ahead. Are you listening to Him? Do you have unquestioning confidence in how He is leading you?

> *Your Good Shepherd understands the path ahead better than you ever could, and He is actively preparing you for it.*

You see, the Father can talk to you all day long, giving you His comfort, guidance, and wisdom. But if you're not willing to hear and act on what He is saying, then what good is it? In the next chapter, we will discuss how to hear and respond to God, but I challenge you right now: *Do not go forward until you're willing to do what He asks of you.*

I say this from experience. There was a time when I was trying to make a decision that would affect many people, and I was having a great deal of difficulty listening to the Lord. I almost made a tremendous mistake.

I had been asked to run for president of the Southern Baptist Convention (SBC), and I have to confess, I didn't want to do it. I felt afraid and inadequate. I was already pastor at First Baptist in Atlanta, so I had my congregation to think of. How could I faithfully minister to them if I focused on leading the

SBC? Also, there was a godly fellow I knew who wanted the position, and I thought he could do a fantastic job. So I fasted and prayed, and I thought I had convinced God that the position was not for me. The night before the election, a group of pastors had a prayer meeting, and they agreed with me that this other man should be president. When I left that night, I thought the burden was off my shoulders.

The day of the election, I woke up feeling fantastic. I got ready as usual and walked to the door. When I reached for the doorknob, the Spirit of God stopped me in my tracks. The Lord said to me, "Don't put your hand on that doorknob until you're willing to do what I ask." His voice was very loud—not in the verbal sense but in its power. I fell on my face at the end of the bed and wept. I was overwhelmed with the understanding that I was at a tremendous fork in the road—with one path that led toward God's will and blessing and the other away from Him. It was like the Lord was saying, "Here is your choice: You can do as I tell you and discover all the amazing things I desire to accomplish through you, or you can disobey Me and spend the rest of your life wondering what I could have done if you had submitted to My plan."

I said, "Lord, I still don't want to do this. I'm afraid! But Father, if that's what You want, I am willing to obey. I don't want to miss Your best for my life. So no matter how big a failure I am, the answer is yes." Now, I didn't know whether I was going to win, or whether I would lose and be completely humiliated in front of everyone. All I knew was that God was calling me, and I needed to be obedient.

That became a momentous event in my life—not because of the position I was elected to but because I decided once and for all that regardless of the cost or consequences, I would obey the Father. The truth of the matter is that God is asking you to make the same decision.

Decide once and for all that regardless of the cost or consequences, you will obey the Father.

He is saying, "Here is your choice: Do as I instruct, and discover all the astounding things I will accomplish through you, or spend the rest of your life wondering what I could have done if you had submitted to My wonderful plans."

The Lord wants to communicate with you. He will speak to you about the critical issues in your life that have you worried and confused. He knows exactly how to handle them and how to enable you to make the best decisions for you and your loved ones.

Will you listen to Him? Will you say yes to Him no matter what your fears are or what consequences may arise? I pray you will, because your Good Shepherd will lead you to life at its best.

―――

Father, how grateful we are that You are our Shepherd, and we can have confidence in all that You tell us. We thank You for speaking to us, Lord—for drawing us into a conversation, speaking to us about Your plans for our lives, revealing Your-self to us, and confirming what You would like to do in and through us. Thank You for giving us the victory whenever we walk in obedience to Your will and Your ways.

Father, we claim the promise of Exodus 15:13: "In Your loving-kindness You have led the people whom You have re-deemed." As this dear reader seeks to know You better and learns the sound of Your voice, I pray You will make Yourself known in a powerful way. Fill this soul with the knowledge of Your will in all spiritual wisdom and understanding. Help this individual to wait on Your perfect timing, trust You every step of the way, and be willing to obey all You ask.

In Jesus' matchless and majestic name, I pray. Amen.

4

LISTENING TO GOD— WALKING WITH GOD

The Importance of Learning the Sound of His Voice

ON A TRIP I ONCE took to Israel, I witnessed one of the most powerful illustrations of listening to our Good Shepherd that I have ever seen. I will never forget it.

The evening sun was setting, and two shepherds approached a nearby well with their flocks. For approximately twenty minutes, the two men chatted while their sheep mingled and roamed about. The animals wandered everywhere. Soon you could not tell one group from the other because they were so interspersed and scattered throughout the countryside.

Then something extraordinary happened. One of the shepherds turned around, quietly called out a command, and started walking away. Instantly, those two flocks separated. The sheep recognized their master's voice, and as he made his way up the hillside, they streamed in from every direction to follow him. They knew exactly what to do and were motivated to obey.

This is the relationship that the Bible tells us we can have with the Lord Jesus—we can become so accustomed and attuned to His voice that we will recognize Him, regardless of all the other messages competing for our attention. As we saw in the last chapter, Jesus affirmed, "My sheep hear My voice, and I know them, and they follow Me" (John 10:27). In Jeremiah 7:23, the Lord says, "Obey My voice, and I will be your God, and you will be My people; and you will walk in all the way which I command you, that it may be well with you."

We can become so accustomed and attuned to His voice that we will recognize Him, regardless of all the other messages competing for our attention.

In other words, if we believe in Jesus as our Savior, then we *will* recognize His call and have the capacity to know the One who saves us. We will be able to walk in the wonderful paths He has for our lives and experience the best He has to offer.

Let me ask you: Can you identify the Shepherd's voice? When the Master speaks to you, do you realize it is His voice? Are you motivated to follow when He summons you?

Listening to God is essential if you want to walk with Him and understand His specific plans for your life. That is why it is so important for you to learn to hear the Father's voice. Once you do, you can engage in the ultimate conversation and have an intimate relationship with Him. Perhaps the first, most crucial step in doing so is becoming an active, attentive, and purposeful listener.

ACTIVELY PURSUING HIS VOICE

Years ago, a dear friend of mine taught me the principle of being aware of God's instructive voice in every situation. He was a godly pastor, and each time I heard him preach, the Lord spoke to me powerfully, as if the message were specifically for me. As you can imagine, I looked forward to hearing my friend's sermons with immense interest because I knew the Father would show me something important through him. Whether I longed for insight into a struggle, direction for my life, or inspiration for my faith, I trusted I would hear exactly what was needed because God consistently spoke through him. Therefore, I always listened eagerly and attentively.

Being a godly man, my friend pointed out that if we anticipate that the Father will speak through a preacher or teacher, we will always receive something from their messages. This is because we're focused on the Lord and paying attention to what He is communicating to us. What is crucial for us to understand is that God is constantly teaching us—patiently demonstrating His love and wisdom to us through every event and detail of our lives. Our challenge is to *expect* Him to reveal Himself with an open and willing heart, regardless of what we're facing, and *intentionally apply* what He says.

> *God is constantly teaching us—patiently demonstrating His love and wisdom to us through every event and detail of our lives.*

Throughout the years, I've found this principle to be absolutely true and foundational to our personal relationships with the Lord. Most of us go through life thinking, *If God has something to say to me, He will make it apparent.* We have a passive attitude when interacting with the Father. We don't take into account that the Lord wants us to hear Him and is continuously speaking messages of wisdom, hope, and instruction to us.

But He is. If we can make this shift in the way we listen to Him, it will radically transform our relationships with Him.

I would like you to think deeply about this truth because I believe it will make a tremendous difference in your life, especially if you are having difficulty hearing the Father: God speaks to you and me through *every* situation, *but hearing Him is dependent upon our anticipating and paying attention to His instruction.*

The Lord has something to say to me, and I'm not going to miss it!

In order to listen to the Father, we must persistently be of this mind-set: *The Lord has something to say to me, and I'm not going to miss it!* Regardless of the circumstances we experience, we know God is teaching us something, and we will intentionally and eagerly learn and apply whatever it is.

LEARNING TO IDENTIFY HIS VOICE

I was motivated to learn about the Father's voice very early in life. My grandfather would tell me how God was speaking to him, and his words created an incredible desire within me for the Lord's presence. I longed for Him to communicate with me as well.

Perhaps you have the same yearning, and you wonder, *What is necessary for us to learn to listen to Him?* Maybe you've heard God in the past but suddenly find Him silent and unresponsive. It's also possible you hear testimonies about people receiving His divine guidance, experiencing His love, and being blessed by His provision, but you don't understand how to recognize the Lord's voice for yourself. What can you do?

AN IMPORTANT STARTING PLACE: GOD'S WORD

The best place you can begin to learn God's voice is through His Word. King David proclaimed, "Your word is a lamp to my feet and a light to my path" (Ps. 119:105). The Bible contains the Lord's plans and principles for living. It is the written record of His unfolding revelation throughout history—of His ways, character, and nature.

We have all been in situations where we could hear other people speaking but could not see their faces. Perhaps they were on the radio, in another office, or outside. As we listened, we knew exactly who was talking because we recognized the tone of voice, the turn of speech, the focus of the message, or even the sound of the laughter.

This is what Scripture does for us: It familiarizes us with *what* God says and *how* He communicates it to us. It trains us to hear His voice. If you truly want to know how to listen to the Father's voice, the best way is to study His Word.

> *Scripture familiarizes us with what God says and how He communicates it to us. It trains us to hear His voice.*

1. It Reveals God's Ways

First, when you read Scripture, you are receiving the Lord's very thoughts into your own mind. Through it, you discover how the Father solves problems, works in and through people, moves on behalf of those who trust Him, responds in different situations, and interacts with all of creation. It is an awesome guidebook that teaches you the ways and character of the living Lord. You learn who He is and how much He loves you (John 1:1; 14).

2. It Is Your Guardrail

Second, the Bible is helpful because you know the Father will never instruct you to do anything that contradicts His Word. If you believe He is telling you something, you can always go back to Scripture and find either confirmation or further direction (Ps. 119:11–12).

3. It Comforts You

Third, God's Word calms the anxious heart. It is amazing how reading about the Lord's redemptive and loving activity throughout history can give a person hope and confidence. Through Scripture, the Father counteracts any wrong opinion you or I may have of Him and reinforces the fact that He is fully trustworthy (Rom. 15:4).

4. It Reminds You of God's Commitment to You

Fourth, the Bible assures you of the Lord's presence, power, and provision in your life—the promises you need most in order to have confidence in Him. It reminds you of who it is you are counting on.

The Lord God Almighty, your heavenly Father:

- "Goes ahead of you; He will be with you. He will not fail you or forsake you. Do not fear or be dismayed." (Deut. 31:8)
- "Is near to the brokenhearted and saves those who are crushed in spirit." (Ps. 34:18)
- Says, "Do not fear, for I am with you; do not anxiously look about you, for I am your God. I will strengthen you, surely I will help you, surely I will uphold you with My righteous right hand." (Isa. 41:10)

- Has "loved you with an everlasting love" and has "drawn you with loving-kindness." (Jer. 31:3)
- "Is in your midst, a victorious warrior. He will exult over you with joy, He will be quiet in His love, He will rejoice over you with shouts of joy." (Zeph. 3:17)

5. It Convicts You of Sin

Fifth, God's Word reveals the places in your life that are preventing you from hearing the Father's voice. At times we know the Lord is speaking to us, but we're afraid or unwilling to listen because of the pain we believe it may cause us. However, as you study Scripture, the Holy Spirit works on you, increasing your discomfort in the areas you are withholding from Him. He also brings to mind the things you've learned, with the goal of helping you find freedom from any bondage that remains in your life (Heb. 4:12).

6. It Gives You God's Viewpoint

Finally, the Bible teaches you how to think as the Father thinks and helps you to see your circumstances from His perspective. Nothing in your life is an accident—there is no such thing as luck or chance. We have the assurance "that God causes all things to work together for good to those who love God, to those who are called according to *His* purpose" (Rom. 8:28). As challenges and obstacles arise in our lives, we know the

Lord wants to speak to us about why He has allowed them and what He will accomplish through them.

For example, I once took a mission trip to New Zealand, and the pastor asked me to speak to several groups of businesspeople. What he did not tell me was that I was going to preach eight times in one morning. Each session was approximately thirty minutes long.

I tried to take a break between each meeting so I could keep my energy up. However, the room they gave me to rest in was absolutely bare, with not even a chair or bench to sit on—just the concrete floor.

I recall that it was as cold as it could be, and I was having doubts about whether or not I could make it through the sessions. I wrapped myself up in my overcoat, put the Bible under my head, and lay down on the concrete floor.

As I prayed, the Father brought Isaiah 40:31 to mind: "Those who wait for the LORD will gain new strength; they will mount up *with* wings like eagles, they will run and not get tired, they will walk and not become weary."

That verse from Isaiah helped me to realize that the Father never intended me to preach in my own power. He energizes us to do the work He has for us.

So I responded, "Lord, I'm already a little bit tired, but I am waiting on You. God, You promised that if I would trust You, You would provide me with Your energy and power. I can't do this on my own, Father. But I have faith You will speak to these people through me."

Wouldn't you know it—I preached all eight times and when I finished, I wasn't even tired. The Lord used Isaiah 40:31 to again teach me that He takes full responsibility for our needs when we obey Him.

As challenges and obstacles arise, we know the Lord wants to speak to us about why He has allowed them and what He will accomplish through them.

MAKING THE MOST OF YOUR TIME IN THE WORD

Therefore, as you read Scripture, there is a great deal you can look forward to in terms of hearing the Father. Here are a few things you can do to make your time with Him as effective as possible.

1. Meditate on the Word

This means not just reading a passage of Scripture but actively thinking about what it means. I've discovered that if I study a particular verse and God brings me back to it the next morning, He is saying something important to me. There are sections of the Bible that I've wrestled with for days and weeks until the Lord helped me understand what He was teaching me. Take your time and allow the truth of God's Word to sink deep into your heart. For example, let us look at Psalm 1:

How blessed is the man who does not walk in the
   counsel of the wicked,
Nor stand in the path of sinners,
Nor sit in the seat of scoffers!
But his delight is in the law of the LORD,
And in His law he meditates day and night.
He will be like a tree *firmly* planted by streams of
   water,
Which yields its fruit in its season
And its leaf does not wither;
And in whatever he does, he prospers.

The wicked are not so,
But they are like chaff which the wind drives away.
Therefore the wicked will not stand in the judgment,
Nor sinners in the assembly of the righteous.
For the LORD knows the way of the righteous,
But the way of the wicked will perish. (vv. 1–6)

Of course, the message of Psalm 1 is that we must live
a life of obedience. Can you think of an example of stand-
ing "in the path of sinners" or sitting "in the seat of scoffers"? (v. 1). What are modern-day examples of these activities?
How would it help you to "be like a tree firmly planted by
streams of water"? (v. 3). What does it mean to be "like chaff
which the wind drives away"? (v. 4).

By asking these and similar questions, you dive deeper into
the meaning of the passage. You may even wish to do some

research to enhance your understanding of what the verses meant when they were originally written.

2. Anticipate That God Will Meet You in a Personal Way

As we said at the beginning of the chapter, it is of utmost importance that you *expect* the Father to speak to you intimately and purposefully through the verses you've read. Actively seek out what He is teaching you.

For example, in reading Psalm 1, you may ascertain that God's desire is to confirm you are pleasing in His sight. Or maybe He reveals that you're associating with people who are hurting your relationship with Him.

The point is, if you examine Scripture with the anticipation and intention of hearing God, you will be amazed at what He shows you and how He transforms your life.

3. Pray That the Lord Will Show You How to Apply It

As you consider the passage you've read, ask, "What are You saying to me, Lord?"

As you consider the passage you've read, ask the Father, "What are You saying to me, Lord? How does this verse relate to my life? Is there something I need to change in order to follow You more closely?"

As you pray, more questions may come to mind. Perhaps you read the line "yields its fruit in its season" (v. 3) and wonder if you are producing the harvest God intends for you to bear. This motivates you to ask the Father whether you're focusing your energy on the right activities or if there are other opportunities to serve that He would like you to explore.

Maybe you read "the wicked will not stand in the judgment" (v. 5) and a lost family member comes to mind. Immediately, you feel the need to pray for him and tell him about Jesus.

As you think about the passage, the Holy Spirit will examine your heart and bring to the surface the issues He wants you to deal with.

Do not be surprised by the questions and concerns that arise. As you intentionally think about the passage and listen with purpose to the Father, the Holy Spirit will examine your heart and bring to the surface the issues He wants you to deal with.

4. Be Prepared to Obey Whatever the Lord Tells You to Do

The next step is to submit to whatever the Father asks of you, then act on what you've heard. You may find this difficult at times. As a matter of fact, what the Lord instructs you to do may not make sense to you. Obey Him anyway.

God does not require you and me to understand His will, just to obey it, even if it seems unreasonable. This is because His goal is to grow your faith and draw you into a closer relationship with Him. I'm sure if you could see this act of obedience in light of His entire will for your life, it would make complete sense. But the Lord reveals the path He has for your life only one step at a time so you can learn to trust Him.

Thankfully, James 1:25 promises us: "One who looks intently at the perfect law, the law of liberty, and abides by it, not having become a forgetful hearer but an effectual doer, this man will be blessed in what he does." In other words, as you hear and do what the Lord says, He rewards your faithfulness.

5. Be Willing to Wait

Finally, be patient with yourself and with the Father. As I said, there have been instances when it took me weeks to fully understand what the Lord was teaching me through a passage of Scripture. There are many lessons—such as faith—that can be learned only with time. Always remember the lesson God taught me on that concrete floor in New Zealand: "Those who wait for the LORD will gain new strength; they will mount up *with* wings like eagles, they will run and not get tired, they will walk and not become weary" (Isa. 40:31).

As you wait patiently for the Father, He is making you stronger, building you up, and working on your behalf.

As you wait patiently for the Father, He is making you stronger, building you up, and working on your behalf. And as you actively seek and listen to God, you will not only hear His voice more often; your life will change in an amazing way.

OTHER WAYS WE HEAR HIS VOICE

Reading God's Word is not the only way to listen to the Lord. Although I encourage you to have Scripture open as you talk with Him, you can hear the Father's voice in other ways as well.

1. Through Worship and Praise

Sometimes you and I just need to set aside time to think about who God is, asking Him to reveal Himself to us in new ways. We sing about His excellent character, praise Him, recall His blessings, and give Him thanks for the good things He's done on our behalf. We honor the Father, grateful for how He works in each of our lives.

Why do we do so? Psalm 95:6–9 admonishes:

Come, let us worship and bow down,
Let us kneel before the LORD our Maker.
For He is our God,
And we are the people of His pasture and the sheep of
    His hand.
Today, if you would hear His voice,

Do not harden your hearts, as at Meribah,
As in the day of Massah in the wilderness,
"When your fathers tested Me,
They tried Me, though they had seen My work."

Here we see that having a healthy reverence for God is important because it keeps us from doubting His goodness and provision, as the nation of Israel did at Meribah (Ex. 17:1–7).

Having a healthy reverence for God is important because it keeps us from doubting His goodness and provision.

The Father had faithfully and miraculously delivered the people out of Egyptian bondage. However, as they wandered in the wilderness, they began grumbling, asking for water and showing complete disrespect toward the Lord. They said, "Why, now, have you brought us up from Egypt, to kill us and our children and our livestock with thirst?" (v. 3).

As we face trials and challenges, we may likewise be tempted to question the Father's purposes if we are not worshiping Him regularly. However, these times of exalting Him reset our thinking, helping us recognize that He is the Source of all we have and our Defender in every situation. Then, instead of doubting Him when difficulties arise, we learn to listen to Him even more closely.

Therefore, if you would like to hear the Father and increase your intimacy with Him, you must make time for praise and worship (Rom. 12:1).

2. Through Circumstances

We can also hear God's voice through the details of everyday life. Whether we lose a job, experience some kind of conflict or challenge, or simply encounter an open door, the Father may be trying to teach us something.

One summer I was up in the mountains of North Carolina on vacation when a deacon from a local church asked me to preach. Their pastor was away on vacation, and they couldn't find anyone to fill the pulpit while he was gone. I knew nothing about the church or the community, but I agreed. That Sunday I preached, and they liked how I taught God's Word, so they invited me back.

That turned out to be the first congregation I would lead on my own Fruitland Baptist Church. Their pastor, Noah Abraham Melton, had been there for forty-seven years and wished to retire, and they wanted someone trustworthy to take his place. The Father showed them during the vacation that I was the man for the job. So they waited a year for me to finish seminary, and then they asked me to be their pastor.

The point is, God engineers the details of our lives to suit His plans and purposes. If you listen to Him, you can hear Him speaking to you through each event, no matter how big or small.

> *God engineers the details of our lives to suit His plans and purposes.*

3. *Through Godly Counsel*

We can often hear God's voice through other people as well—they help us understand what He is doing in our lives, hold us accountable, and encourage us to follow Him in obedience (Heb. 10:24–25). Proverbs 1:5 tells us, "A wise man will hear and increase in learning, and a man of understanding will acquire wise counsel."

However, before taking advice from anyone, be sure to consider: *Is this person living an obedient, godly life? Can I trust this individual to listen to the Lord?*

Also, never say: "What do *you* think I should do?" Instead, always ask: "What does the *Word of God* say I should do?" This takes the emphasis off of another person's opinion and places it on the Lord's direction, where it should be.

The Father can encourage and edify you greatly through others. Just be sure you are speaking to people who place Him first and have your best interests at heart.

4. *Through Your Conscience*

Your conscience is a gift from God, given to protect you from engaging in behaviors that could ultimately destroy you. It is the moral capacity that enables you to distinguish right from wrong, as well as between what is good and what is best for your life. When submitted to the Holy Spirit, your conscience can be a powerful vessel through which the Father communicates with you.

If you are wondering whether your conscience should be your guide, allow me to give you this word of caution: Although the Lord *can* speak to you through your conscience, you must be very careful to train it to respond in a godly manner that honors Him. You do that by always setting the Word of God as your standard for living, surrendering to the Holy Spirit, and confessing and repenting of sin as soon as you are aware of it.

When submitted to the Holy Spirit, your conscience can be a powerful way through which the Father communicates with you.

You see, the conscience is weakened and defiled if we engage in ungodly behaviors and ignore the Holy Spirit's admonitions to stop what we're doing. Eventually, a conscience can grow so accustomed to disregarding the Lord's warnings that it loses all sensitivity to His promptings.

If we want to hear God, it is crucial to keep our conscience blameless before Him by cleansing it with His Word.

5. Through a Restless Spirit

Another way we hear God's voice is through a feeling of agitation or anticipation. Right before every significant change I've experienced in my life, I've felt restless in my spirit. It was the Father's way of getting my attention—of tuning my ears to His voice so I would be prepared to obey His direction.

Whenever you sense yourself becoming agitated or stirred

up inside, get on your knees and ask God, "What are You saying to me, Lord?" Remember that He sends such feelings to
motivate you to pray because He has something important to
show you.

IS SOMETHING KEEPING YOU FROM HEARING THE FATHER?

If you are reading Scripture and praying but having difficulty
hearing God, something in your life may be preventing you
from having the ultimate conversation with Him. At this
point, it is easy to become discouraged.
But don't lose heart. Rest assured that
your heavenly Father has the power and
wisdom to root out whatever is impeding
your relationship with Him.

Your heavenly
Father has
the power and
wisdom to root
out whatever is
impeding your
relationship
with Him.

As we have seen, it is out of character
for the Lord to withhold the truth from
us. He desires to interact with each of us
in a powerful way and is motivated to remove anything that hinders our fellowship with Him.

Therefore, ask God to examine your
heart. Pray about the following questions,
and ask if any of these issues are thwarting you from enjoying
a deep and meaningful conversation with Him.

- Am I intentional and expectant when I engage in a conversation with the Father?
- Do I feel unworthy or undeserving of the Lord's guidance or grace?
- Am I failing to make time for God—forgetting to pray because of less meaningful activities?
- Do I doubt the Father's character or what He has promised?
- Have I already made up my mind about what I want to do, thereby making it difficult to hear God's will?
- Am I being influenced by others who discourage me to obey the Lord like I should?
- Is there someone I should forgive?
- Am I holding on to any wrong opinions about the Father that I should release?
- Is there any area of my life where I am operating by preference rather than godly biblical principles?
- Am I afraid of God's will, thinking it may hurt me or those I love?
- Is there any sin in my life that I must confess?
- Is there anything I am refusing to give up in obedience to the Father?

As you pray, if anything stands out or if you feel convicted about a particular issue, stop right there. Ask God to heal you and show you what to do. He may direct you to talk to someone, read a passage of Scripture, or repent of a behavior that has impeded your relationship with Him. Regardless of what He shows you, agree with Him and obey immediately. Remember, obedience always brings blessing. And there is no greater reward than unhindered fellowship with the Father.

God can and will speak to you in a number of ways. When you know what He wants you to do, don't allow anything to keep you from following His call. Your own plans cannot compare with the good things the Lord has in store for you. Your wisest course of action is always to submit yourself to His will and trust Him to help you.

> *There is no greater reward than unhindered fellowship with the Father.*

A CLOSING THOUGHT

As I wrote previously, God is *constantly* teaching us—patiently demonstrating His love and wisdom to us through every event and detail of our lives. He will reveal Himself if we eagerly anticipate and pay attention to His instruction.

With this in mind, I have always been inspired and amazed by the impressive expanse of the night sky. For years, I would go to my study window every Saturday night and look out at the brightly shining constellations in awe and wonder. One cannot help but see the wisdom, beauty, and majesty of the Father in every part of His creation.

Consider the awesome nature of space—how light travels 186,000 miles a second, and how a star can be trillions of miles away from us, yet we can still see it. The Lord spoke the entire universe into existence and then placed the billions of stars, worlds, and galaxies in their orbits, naming each and every one. Everything that exists—from the smallest particle to the infinity of space —rests in the omnipotent hand of our omniscient Father. He is in perfect control because He is sovereign over the universe. What a mighty and astounding God we serve! We cannot begin to grasp how immense, magnificent, and powerful our Lord God truly is.

These same wonders inspired David to write Psalm 8:

O LORD, our Lord,
How majestic is Your name in all the earth,
Who have displayed Your splendor above the
    heavens! . . .
When I consider Your heavens, the work of
    Your fingers,
The moon and the stars, which You have ordained;
What is man that You take thought of him,
And the son of man that You care for him? (vv. 1, 3–4)

Sometimes it is easy to feel this way: *Lord, who am I that You would bother talking to me? Why should You care about the details of my life?*

Yet God *is* mindful of you. The Good Shepherd watches over the particulars of your life. And He wants you to hear His voice.

> *God is mindful of you. The Good Shepherd watches over the particulars of your life. And He wants you to hear His voice.*

Just remember, the One who keeps the sun, moon, stars, galaxies, and constellations in their places and who maintains the earth rotating at the right speed, on the correct axis, and with the precise amount of oxygen we need in the air is the One who can communicate with you, regardless of what you're going through.

If you are having difficulty hearing the Father, or if there is some question you are longing for Him to answer, don't give up. He wants to talk to you.

Keep seeking His face and listening for His call.

Father, how grateful we are that You are our Good Shepherd who speaks to us in so many ways. What a privilege to know You, Lord—the majestic, wonderful, powerful God of all creation. Thank You for communicating with us and for giving us Your Word so we can learn to hear Your Voice.

Father, I pray for this reader who desires to hear Your call and walk in agreement with You. God, draw this dear person into an intimate relationship with You, teaching this individual how to connect with You in deeper, more meaningful ways than ever before. Give this person a spirit of anticipation and expectancy whenever approaching Your throne of grace. Help Your child to be open, yielded, and available for whatever You desire to do. Thank You for revealing Your ways and making Your voice known to this precious soul.

To You be all the honor, glory, power, and praise. In Jesus' holy and majestic name, I pray. Amen.

5

~

CHRIST'S EXAMPLE
OF INTIMACY

Communicating with the Father as Jesus Would

IN STUDYING THE ULTIMATE CONVERSATION, we have discussed whom we are speaking to; the fact that God has a great deal to say to each of us personally; and the importance of heeding His call. Of course, learning principles and putting them into practice are two different things.

There may be times when it feels as if you cannot say the right thing to God. Perhaps you are uncertain that you've heard His voice, though you strain your ears listening. It may be that your dreams seem lost; the path ahead of you appears vague and unpromising; and you don't understand why God has brought you to this painful and difficult place. You try to communicate with the Father, but like the psalmist Asaph, you feel as if you're doing an unskillful and terrible job. Asaph wrote, "When my heart was embittered and I was pierced within, then I was senseless and ignorant; I was like a beast before You" (Ps. 73:21–22). Sometimes we may feel so clumsy and brutish when talking to God that we wonder if it's any use approaching Him at all.

Thankfully, in all these things, we are especially blessed as believers because we have a living, breathing example of what deep intimacy with the Father looks like through Jesus. In fact, Hebrews 1:1–3 tells us:

> God, after He spoke long ago to the fathers in the prophets in many portions and in many ways, in these last days has spoken to us in His Son, whom He appointed heir of all things, through whom also He made the world. And *He is the radiance of His glory and the exact representation of His nature,* and upholds all things by the word of His power. (emphasis added)

Throughout history, the Lord told us about Himself through the patriarchs, priests, and prophets. In Jesus, God showed us a precise demonstration of who He is. Colossians 1:15 tells us, "He is the image of the invisible God." The indescribably awesome, infinite Lord of all that exists took on a form like ours and dwelled among us so we could know Him better. We have a model for how God interacts with us by studying the life of Jesus.

We have a living, breathing example of what deep intimacy with the Father looks like through Jesus.

Why did He do this? Why did He go through the trouble of becoming a man? Wasn't there another way?

Hebrews 2:17–18 (TLB) explains, "It was necessary for Jesus to be like us, His brothers, so that He could be our merciful and faithful High Priest before God . . . For since He Himself has now been through suffering and temptation, he knows what it is like when we suffer and are tempted, and he is wonderfully able to help us."

Your Savior Jesus knows exactly what you are experiencing. He comprehends the difficult decisions you must make and the inner struggles that often accompany doing the right thing (Luke 22:42). He understands the heartache of being rejected and betrayed by others (Matt. 26:47–56). And He fully recognizes the absolute agony of being forsaken—utterly abandoned and in terrible emotional and physical pain (Matt. 27:46).

> *Jesus not only appreciates what you are feeling, He faithfully walks through each challenge with you and offers rest for your soul.*

Jesus not only appreciates what you are feeling, He faithfully walks through each challenge with you and offers rest for your soul (Matt. 11:29–30).

A CONVERSATION THAT HONORS GOD

Jesus is the perfect One to teach us how to have a meaningful conversation with the Father. As He does so, there are two things we can count on:

First, because Jesus is *fully God* (John 1:1; 10:30), He shows us how to address Him in a way that honors Him and brings Him glory. The Lord is clear about what He expects from us.

Second, being *fully man* (Phil. 2:5–8; Heb. 2:14–18), Jesus profoundly understands what we're experiencing and demonstrates how to pray in a way that best meets our needs and ministers to our spirits.

Sometimes we make our conversations with the Father much more complicated than they need to be. Sadly, we don't enjoy all the blessings of being in His awesome presence. But in Jesus, we see that interacting with God does not have to be challenging or confusing. Therefore, we are going to look in depth at the Savior's pattern of prayer to find out how we can talk to God in a way that best pleases Him and helps us.

In Matthew 6:5–13, Jesus instructs,

"When you pray, you are not to be like the hypocrites; for they love to stand and pray in the synagogues and on the street corners so that they may be seen by men. Truly I say to you, they have their reward in full. When you pray, go into your inner room, close your door and pray to your Father who is in secret, and your Father who sees what is done in secret will reward you.

"And when you are praying, do not use meaningless repetition as the Gentiles do, for they suppose that they will be heard for their many words. So do not be like them; for your Father knows what you need before you ask Him.

"Pray, then, in this way:

'Our Father who is in heaven,
Hallowed be Your name.
'Your kingdom come.
Your will be done,
On earth as it is in heaven.
'Give us this day our daily bread.
'And forgive us our debts, as we also have forgiven
   our debtors.
'And do not lead us into temptation, but deliver us
   from evil.
[For Yours is the kingdom and the power and the
   glory forever. Amen.']"

Close the Door

The first thing you and I should see from Jesus' instruction is that He wants us all to Himself. He says, "You are not to be like the hypocrites; for they love to stand and pray in the synagogues and on the street corners so that they may be seen by men. . . . When you pray, go into your inner room, close your door and pray" (Matt. 6:5–6). We should have periods of interaction with the Father when there is no one else around; when we can be unhurried, undistracted, uninterrupted, and deliberate in spending time with Him.

Therefore, as *fully God,* Jesus communicates what He desires from us: our complete, unimpeded attention. He wants us to choose Him above the cares and activities of our days and acknowledge Him as Lord of our lives. As *fully man,* the

Savior understands how imperative it is for us daily to have our concerns heard, sins forgiven, fears calmed, hearts encouraged, and souls renewed.

We see this modeled throughout Jesus' life. Mark 1:35 reports, "In the early morning, while it was still dark, Jesus got up, left the house, and went away to a secluded place, and was praying there." Matthew 14:23 tells us that on a different occasion, "He went up on the mountain by Himself to pray; and when it was evening, He was there alone." Jesus understood the importance of frequently engaging in private, unhindered conversation with the Father.

That doesn't mean we should avoid occasions of public intercession. On the contrary, those are important as well (Heb. 10:25). Rather, we should realize we are free to communicate one-on-one with Him and should do so often. The Lord wants us to have the privilege of expressing our feelings, desires, burdens, sorrows, and cares to Him. However, God also wants us to focus on Him, adoring and worshipping Him and allowing Him to love us in return.

God wants us to focus on Him, adoring and worshipping Him and allowing Him to love us in return.

Let me ask you: How much time in any twenty-four-hour period does God have your undivided attention? How often does the Lord have you all to Himself? If you're affording a few minutes to the Father—making your requests and then hurrying on your way—you're not really praying. That is not genuine communion or fellowship.

Think about two young people who are falling in love. They don't fill up their day with meaningless activity and avoid each other. They make time to interact and demonstrate to each other how much they care.

Why don't we treat the Lord the same way? Why don't we rush to see Him—disregarding everything else that is going on—and tell Him how grateful we are for His wonderful care and perfect provision? Until we choose to spend time alone with God and allow Him to energize us with His presence, we will never truly understand the power of having a conversation with Him. When we do, we will long for constant communion with the Father because we will understand what an immense privilege it is.

Secret and Sincere

The second thing we need is the mind-set we should have when speaking with the Lord. Jesus said, "Pray to your Father who is in secret, and your Father who sees what is done in secret will reward you. And when you are praying, do not use meaningless repetition as the Gentiles do, for they suppose that they will be heard for their many words. So do not be like them; for your Father knows what you need before you ask Him" (Matt. 6:6–8).

The crowd Jesus addressed understood that, in telling them to pray in secret, He was not calling them to forsake the public practice of morning (*Shacharit*), afternoon (*Minchah*), and evening (*Ma'ariv*) prayers that accompanied the three daily sacrifices (Ps. 55:17; Dan. 6:10). Rather, He was calling them to test their hearts. What were their motives for calling out to God? Was it out of adoration for the Lord or another purpose?

There were many in that day who made an outward show of their piety—not so much out of love for the Father but because they wanted approval, respect, and power over others. Many of the religious leaders enslaved people with laws and rules, making them believe that salvation must be earned. Jesus denounced their practices in Matthew 23:

> "The scribes and the Pharisees . . . tie up heavy burdens and lay them on men's shoulders, but they themselves are unwilling to move them with *so much as* a finger. But they do all their deeds to be noticed by men; for they broaden their phylacteries and lengthen the tassels *of their garments.* They love the place of honor at banquets and the chief seats in the synagogues. . . .
>
> "But woe to you, scribes and Pharisees, hypocrites, because you shut off the kingdom of heaven from people; for you do not enter in yourselves, nor do you allow those who are entering to go in. . . .
>
> "Woe to you, scribes and Pharisees, hypocrites! For you are like whitewashed tombs which on the outside appear beautiful, but inside they are full of dead men's bones and all uncleanness. So you, too, outwardly appear righteous to men, but inwardly you are full of hypocrisy and lawlessness." (vv. 2, 4–6, 13, 27–28)

These religious leaders were making a mess of things. In their pursuit of prominence through acts of righteousness, they had become prideful, trusting in their own works, rather than in ongoing relationships with the Father.

In a sense, it is a trap we are all in danger of falling into. Many of those Pharisees most likely had a sincere desire to know and serve God, so they practiced the disciplines that were supposed to bring them closer to Him. Eventually, the deeds themselves became more important than the Lord, and that was when they got into trouble.

Likewise, we may be tempted to choose safe acts of devotion over unpredictable lives of service to Almighty God. After all, a living and active relationship with the Lord caused Abraham to leave his home and family in Ur of the Chaldees to settle in Canaan; prompted Moses to confront Pharaoh and lead the Israelites back to the Promised Land; inspired David to challenge the giant Goliath and build the kingdom of Israel; and moved Nehemiah to rebuild the walls of Jerusalem. It is much easier and more comfortable to abide by a set of rules and regulations than to truly know and obey the Father (Matt. 7:21–23). However, it is nowhere near as fulfilling, and it eventually puts us in terrible bondage.

Sadly, the scribes and Pharisees were destroying people's lives by their examples—teaching them that keeping every jot and tittle of the law was the only way to God, rather than demonstrating the justice, mercy, and faithfulness inherent in His commandments. Not only were the people discouraged, they were also prevented from experiencing the loving relationship with the Lord that they longed to have.

That isn't what the Savior wanted for them, and He does not desire it for us, either. As *fully God,* Jesus teaches us the attitude that is appropriate in His presence: We are to seek Him privately, humbly, sincerely, and obediently as dearly loved children, without a thought as to what others may think.

As *fully man,* Jesus sets us free from the burdens of religion that are difficult to bear. We do not have to beg for His attention or put on a show. The Savior wants us to come to Him unguarded and without fear because He loves and accepts us just as we are.

> *We don't need to impress God because He already loves us and knows what we need. He just asks for our open and honest hearts.*

So He instructs us to pray in secret and be sincere, telling Him exactly how we feel. No pretense. No big words. No remarkable demonstrations of how spiritual we are or how much of the Bible we know. We don't need to impress God because He already loves us and knows what we need. We aren't informing Him of anything. He just asks for the opportunity to reveal Himself to our open and honest hearts.

Consequently, we do well to test our motives when we approach Him. We should consider the following questions, asking the Father to reveal any areas where we are not sincere about knowing Him:

- Do we pray to convince others of our godliness?
- Do we ever tell others about our quiet times in order to appear more spiritually mature?
- Do we approach intercession as a ritual we perform to appease the Lord or earn our way to heaven?
- Have our prayers become formulaic and routine, something we simply try to get through?
- Do we pray because there are things that we want the Father to give us? Or do we go to His throne of grace to know Him?
- Are our relationships with the Father more important than the things we are asking Him to provide?
- Do we use repetitive words, hoping we will be heard or that God will give in to our requests?
- Are we trying to convince the Lord to do things our way? Or are we genuinely interested in how He wants us to live?

Remember, " 'GOD IS OPPOSED TO THE PROUD, BUT GIVES GRACE TO THE HUMBLE.' Submit therefore to God. . . . Humble yourselves in the presence of the Lord, and He will exalt you" (James 4:6–7, 10). Always approach the Father respectfully and sincerely, trusting that His love and acceptance are the greatest blessings you can ever receive.

To Repeat or Not to Repeat

Before we move on to the Lord's pattern of communication, there are three things I would like to clarify concerning Jesus' teaching us about repetitive prayer. He said, "When you are praying, do not use meaningless repetition as the Gentiles do" (Matt. 6:7).

*First, this does not mean we will never
repeat our requests to the Father.*
On the contrary, Jesus taught that persistence is important and "at all times [we] ought to pray and not to lose heart" (Luke 18:1). Sometimes we need to be tenacious in our petitions, especially if they are about the salvation of loved ones. God uses those requests to teach us how to watch for His activity and opportunities.

*Second, "meaningless repetition" doesn't mean we
can't say the same words more than once.*
Matthew 26 tells us that in the Garden of Gethsemane, Christ prayed, "My Father, if it is possible, let this cup pass from Me; yet not as I will, but as You will" (v. 39). Verse 42 says, "He went away again a second time and prayed, saying, 'My Father, if this cannot pass away unless I drink it, Your will be done.'" Verse 44 reports, "He left them again, and went away and prayed a third time, saying the same thing once more."

We may often ask the Father for the same thing. There may be sleepless nights when all we know is to cry out, "God, please help me know what to do." Perhaps there will be times when we are fearful, so we recite Psalm 23 or some other passage of Scripture that comforts our hearts. There is nothing wrong with that.

What Jesus was addressing was a common pagan practice that called for continual, rote reiteration of chants that meant nothing to those saying them. They babbled in this manner to increase the likelihood that their deities would respond to their requests.

Consider: If what you're saying to God doesn't express what's in your heart or help you draw closer to Him, what good is it?

> *If what you're saying to God doesn't express what's in your heart or help you draw closer to Him, what good is it?*

Third, Jesus' pattern for speaking with our heavenly Father is just that—a model of conversation.

It is not a magical incantation that we should recite repeatedly without thinking about it. Jesus has given us the prayer so we will feel comfortable interacting with God and address Him in the appropriate manner. To state it mindlessly would be to participate in the meaningless repetition Jesus spoke against.

OUR FATHER IN HEAVEN

As we come to Jesus' pattern for our interaction with God, He begins by saying, "Pray, then, in this way: 'Our Father who is

in heaven'" (Matt. 6:9). What an incredible statement: Jesus—
God incarnate—desires for us to call God *Father!* The Lord of
all creation wants us to be His children and have a very special
relationship with Him.

Fully God, Jesus is expressing God's
intention—He wants this level of intimacy with us. He wants to be our tender

> *Jesus—God
> incarnate—desires
> for us to call
> God Father!*

heavenly Father who loves, teaches, and
provides for us faithfully. And *fully man,*
Jesus realizes how crucial it is for us to be
able to rely upon the Father as a trusting
child relies on his or her strong, wise, and
godly dad.

Perhaps this is a strange idea to you. If so, you're not alone;
it's a foreign concept to many people. It was a revolutionary
view to the Jews of Jesus' day. In the Old Testament, the Lord
is referred to as "Father" only fifteen times—and even those
few instances are primarily in regard to the nation of Israel.

However, Jesus consistently called God "Father," signify-
ing the relationship He wanted us to have with Him. John
1:12 affirms, "As many as received Him, to them He gave the
right to become children of God." Also, Galatians 3:26 tells
us, "You are all sons of God through faith in Christ Jesus."

Maybe the word "father" has negative connotations that
you prefer not to consider, and you dislike using it in reference to God. This often happens when a dad is abusive or
absent, and it can take years for people to recover from what
they experienced during childhood.

Or maybe you had a great dad and have no problem calling the Lord "Father," but you feel as if your relationship with Him is not all it could be. Whether you realize it or not, your earthly father may have something to do with the barriers you have to knowing God.

The truth of the matter is, our understanding of the Lord is directly affected by how we relate to our earthly dads. Even those who have been raised by godly fathers may subconsciously ascribe their dad's limitations, faults, and failures to God. Our first awareness of authority, love, provision, and security comes from our parents. It is only natural that how we perceive them would influence our view of all our relationships, including the one we have with the Lord.

God As My Father

As I told you earlier, my father, Charley Stanley, died in 1933 when I was only nine months old, and his loss affected me greatly. Without realizing it I started life feeling abandoned by a person of great value to me whom I had never met. As earnest and attentive as she was, my mother could not replace the firm guiding hand of the father I did not have. I had entered the world without a reference point. There was never going to be the older and wiser version of me to look to for knowledge, direction, or compassion. I would have to go it alone and figure life out for myself.

Thank goodness my mother was a firm believer in church attendance. Every Sunday morning the other pair of pants

I owned was neatly pressed and ready for the short walk to church and Sunday school. At church, I was told that God loved me and that He was my heavenly Father. I took the minister's word for it, but I always left feeling the same— lonely and vulnerable.

My mother was convinced of the Lord's love and paternal presence, however, and every night before I went to sleep we got down on our knees and talked to the Father as if He really cared and was interested in the details of our lives. I learned how to talk to the Lord before I actually believed in Him by listening to my mother pour out her heart and make requests that she expected to be heard and answered. Further, I became convinced of His existence when our prayers were indeed answered in ways that were unexplainable.

Later in life it occurred to me that, in her own way, my mother was introducing me to the only Person who could ever replace the father I would never have. Unlike her, I was not sure I wanted to know this God who had taken from us too soon the love of her life and the father I desperately longed for. I was not convinced I could count on the Lord, upon whom my mother had come to depend for every dime we spent and for all the basement apartments and rented rooms we would eventually call home. In spite of my doubts, which were fed by an insatiable hunger for something I could not name, the God of my mother's Bible—who claimed *nothing* could separate me from His love—had begun a relentless pursuit of my heart that would not end until the day I surrendered my life to Him.

• • •

So who is this Father God who pursues us and wants to have a relationship with us? As we have seen in the Bible, God has given Himself many names so that we can discover who He is, what His character is like, and what His intentions are toward us.

For instance, we learned in Chapter 2 that God is called *Elohim*, which means "Creator, Preserver, One who is Mighty and Strong." *Elohim* reveals our origin with the assurance that the Father is able to sustain us and protect us. Likewise, we've discussed that He is called *Yahweh*, the self-existent One, because He has always been and will always be. The name *Yahweh* assures us that He will never leave or abandon us.

In Psalm 71, He is called *Kadosh,* which means "Holy One." Because God is holy He cannot sin, and therefore He will never harm His creation. We can rest assured that He will always love us appropriately.

In the book of Job He is called *El Shaddai,* the "All Sufficient One and Almighty God." With the Father we have everything we need if we will look to Him to meet our needs and trust His methods and His timing.

There are many more names for the Lord because, as with you and me, there are many facets to His personality. However, my favorite name for God is found in Psalm 68:5. He is called "a father to the fatherless, a defender of widows" (NIV). As I said, I don't know how you feel about calling God your father, but I know this: My mother and I clung to that verse many nights as we knelt by my bed and prayed that He would provide for our needs, whether it was another place to live or a new pair of shoes for a growing boy. And you know what? Not once did He ever fail to answer us.

I realize you might be thinking, "I am not interested in another father. I am still trying to recover from the one I had." Nevertheless, like me, you were born unaware of someone very valuable to you. You were made in His image but you were separated from Him by death. Not His death, however, but your own. Ephesians 2:1 (NIV) says, "As for you, you were dead in your transgressions and sin." We are all born spiritually dead, separated from God. Like it or not, we are all members of a race that offended God whose name is also Righteous Judge.

Judge—that is the picture many of us are raised with. But God is also our Redeemer. Job says, "I know that my Redeemer lives" (Job 19:25). The word *redeem* means to "buy back by paying a price." So what did our heavenly father, the Righteous Judge, do for us? John 3:16 says it best, "God so loved the world, that He gave His only begotten Son, that whoever believes in Him shall not perish, but have eternal life."

We were headed for eternal separation from the Lord and there was nothing we could do to save ourselves. So God sent His Son, Jesus Christ, to accomplish two goals. The first was to show us what God is like so we could know Him and therefore put our trust in Him. Second, but just as important, Christ was sent to die in our place so that we could spend eternity with Him in heaven and never be separated from Him again.

We were in serious trouble and the Lord executed a plan to save us. What father would allow his children to stay in a perilous state if he had the means and the resources to rescue them? I never understood why God wanted to save me until I had children of my own.

When our children were still very young, we would pack up our trailer every summer and head for the undeveloped, pristine beach of Naples, Florida. It was the trip I looked forward to all year because it meant two coveted weeks alone with my family. There was nothing I enjoyed more than just being with my children. It did not matter what we were doing, only that we were doing it together.

What I loved most about being with them were our conversations. I listened with great interest to their thoughts and reactions, and I carefully edited my comments to keep the conversation spontaneous. Throughout the course of the day, whether I was baiting the hook on my son's fishing rod or admiring the perfect sand dollar my daughter found, I purposely talked to them about my own relationship with God and how He was interested in having a relationship with them as well. The thing I wanted to give them most in this world, I could not. I could only introduce them to God and hope that one day they too would yield to His pursuit and come to know Him as I did.

One day dark clouds appeared just as the tide began to

flood the moat of our morning's sand castle. I started to secure our campsite as the wind rattled the coconuts in the palm trees above us. Unaware of the pending storm, my daughter wandered down the beach looking for unusual shells for her growing collection.

As the water engulfed what was left of the castle, I glanced around to find the children. My son was tucking the folding chairs underneath the trailer, but my daughter was nowhere to be seen. For several terrifying minutes I could not see her or know for certain if she could hear my call. I ran as fast as I could in the direction I thought she had gone while my son waited near the trailer in case she appeared.

What if someone had emerged from the forest and grabbed her? I would never forgive myself and silently begged God to save her. The entire sky was gray when I suddenly came upon a deep hole in the sand. Water was flooding in but it was quickly detoured by my determined little girl who was digging furiously for the special shell she had spotted at the bottom.

Overwhelmed with relief, I jumped into the hole and helped her dig until we retrieved the shell. She had no idea of the horror she had caused or the potential danger she was in. Instead, she was delighted for my enthusiastic assistance as we found the precious shell and I lifted her out of the hole and carried her back to the trailer just as it began to pour.

As I lay in bed that night, I struggled to shake off the fear that consumed me as I searched for my only daughter. I thanked God over and over for enabling me to find her and that she had not been harmed. I needed no excuse for my extreme gratitude and love for her. She was my child and I loved her more than my own life the day she was born.

That is how the Father loves us, only more. He created us and decided to love us, period. When Adam disobeyed the Lord's one command in the Garden of Eden and put the rest of mankind at odds with Him, God sent His only Son to explain who He is and to save us from what we are— condemned and in need of a Savior.

Isaiah 63:16 tells us, "You, O LORD, are our Father, our Redeemer from of old is Your name." And of all God's names and attributes, my favorite is *Father,* because like me with my children, He wants to protect us and build a relationship with us so we can know Him. Because if we really get to know Him, we will trust Him; and if we trust Him, we will grow to love Him; and if we love Him, we will obey Him and that always works out for our good.

Well into my adult years, I struggled with the concept of God as my Father—of sensing His love and understanding how He wanted to interact with me. Having never known my own father, I suppose I grew up with a rather large hole in my heart. I could have filled it with many things that would have destroyed me or at the very least distracted me from God's plan for my life. But I didn't and there is only one reason: My mother's insistence on praying with me every night taught me a very valuable lesson I did not even know I was learning.

Consistent, deliberate time alone with God in prayer is not

an option in the Christian life. Nothing takes priority over it, nothing accomplishes more than it, and there is no way to have a real and meaningful relationship with God without it. When I left home, my mom did not have much to send with me. However, she sent me with all that I needed—a prayer life that had become second nature and a faith that was based on real answers to prayer from a real God who cares for me. It is my hope to introduce every person I can to that same heavenly Father, just as my mother did for me.

God was faithful in teaching me what kind of relationship He desired with each of His children. And He can show you, too.

With this in mind, I can assure you— God is absolutely faithful to show us what kind of relationship He desires to have with each of His children. He can show you, too.

What can you and I expect from the Lord as our heavenly Father?

Relationship

God wants to have an ongoing, intimate bond with us, and He has gone to great lengths to provide it (Rom. 8:31–33). Our earthly fathers may reject us and cause us great pain, but not God. He always has time for us (Heb. 4:16), will never fail or forsake us (Heb. 13:5), and unfailingly accepts us (Rom. 15:7). Though we may feel inadequate or unprepared to have an open and loving relationship with the Father because of the past, remember—the One who saves you can teach you how to relate to Him. He will instruct you in how to walk with Him step by step (Ps. 25:4–5).

Unconditional Love

Although parents may make us feel as if we need to earn their approval by meeting certain standards of behavior, performance, beauty, or intelligence, God receives us just as we are (Matt. 9:12–13). He does not compare us with anyone else, and nothing can separate us from His love (Rom. 8:37–39). We can be transparent with Him because we know we'll never lose Him (1 John 4:15–19). If your ability to receive the Father's unconditional love has been damaged because of your past, there is healing for you. He sees your wounds and has a plan to restore you (John 15:9–10). Trust Him.

Communication

As we've been discussing, the Father wants to communicate with us. He wants to reveal Himself, teach us how to love and obey Him, and show us the path to life at its best (Jer. 29:11–13). When He disciplines us, we know it is for our good, to protect us from evil and mature our faith (Heb. 12:7–11). When we long for comfort, assurance, and hope, He restores our soul (Ps. 23). And when we need guidance, He consistently helps us to do the right thing (Prov. 3:5–6). The best part is, we can always trust what He tells us because He has never failed to keep His word (Josh. 21:45). We may have felt misunderstood and alienated by our parents. But no one comprehends us better than our heavenly Father, who knows every aspect and detail of our lives (Ps. 139).

Provision

This is another area where earthly parents may have fallen short and caused us to doubt God. Perhaps your family was poor, like mine was, and you sometimes wondered where your next meal would come from. Or maybe your parents had plenty of income and indulged your every wish, but what you desired most was their time and love. It's possible that your dad was absent somehow, and you feel a lack of security and self-worth. Jesus assures us, "Your Father knows what you need before you ask Him" (Matt. 6:8). God already knows all the areas in our lives that require His touch (Phil. 4:19). He can satisfy whatever physical, emotional, and spiritual necessities we have, and He assumes full responsibility for our needs as we obey Him (Matt. 6:25–26).

> *The Lord has none of the faults or frailties of your earthly father; He is perfect in every way, including how He loves you.*

These descriptions are brief, and if you are struggling with seeing God as your Father, they are only a starting place for you. The Lord has none of the faults or frailties of your earthly father; He is perfect in every way, including how He loves you.

As you continue having the ultimate conversation with Him, I am confident that He will not only show you the truth about His character and care as your heavenly Father; He will also heal any wounds from your childhood. However, you must be willing to deal with the areas He reveals to you and trust Him to mend any brokenness you feel. This requires vulnerability and courage, but take heart: God is never late working in your life. Never allow fear to get in the way of what He wants to accomplish in you.

A PRINCIPLE BEFORE PROCEEDING

In Chapter 6, we will continue discussing the pattern for the ultimate conversation that Jesus taught us. Before we proceed, I urge you not to underestimate the influence your parents had on your life, whether they were present or not. It is important for you to think about this because your relationship with your parents can impact how you view God and life in general.

I recall a fine young man I had the privilege of knowing. He was talented, gifted, and quite handsome. It seemed as if he had everything going for him. But one day he came into my office and sat down to relate some of the difficulties he was having.

I listened as he told me his struggles. Finally, I said, "Why don't we try to find the root of what's going on here?" He agreed. I asked him several questions about his past, and he told me a heartbreaking story.

When this young man was around nine years old, he was in his bedroom and heard his parents arguing in the next room. In the midst of their fight, they began discussing his future and how they felt about him. It was then that he heard the statement that would ultimately shape the rest of his life: "Why should I care? I didn't want him anyway!"

His eyes filled with tears as he repeated it: " 'Why should I care? I didn't want him anyway.' " You and I can imagine how painful it would be for a child to hear such a remark from the very people who were supposed to support and cherish him.

This event drove how this man related to every aspect of his life from then on. He longed to feel as if he were *somebody*. He yearned to be accepted, to prove he was worthy of being loved. And every goal he pursued—college, seminary, a family, a pastorate—was so he could fill the horrible void in his life. But none of it did.

I wish I could say he turned to God and found freedom from that rejection, but I cannot. He was unwilling to allow the Lord to deal with this painful place in his life. Deep down, he believed the enemy's vicious lie that the Father wasn't interested in him, either—that God Himself was saying: "Why should I care? I didn't want him anyway."

He rejected what the Lord was doing in his life. And without God's help, he was never able to stop those words from ringing in his ears. So he lived with that terrible message every day of his life.

Several years later, after a series of devastating events, that bright and talented young man took his own life. It breaks my heart every time I think of him.

Every one of us has a library in our mind of what we've seen, felt, and been told throughout our lives. These memories and events affect how we respond to situations and circumstances, whether we're aware of it or not.

One of my earliest memories is from when I was two or three years old. I recall sitting on a bed in a room with old wooden walls and a kerosene lamp. It was dark, and I was crying because I had an earache and there was no one to take care of me; my mother was at work. Being alone at such a young age made me feel frightened and insecure. Eight decades later, I remember that experience clearly, and I can see how it has impacted my life and ministry.

What events and statements do you recall? What words and memories have shaped how you live? Maybe you have endured some difficult trials and weathered them successfully. However, you should never underestimate the damage they may have done. You cannot just forget the challenges that occurred in your youth— they will continue to surface, no matter how far you attempt to push them out of your mind.

There are three senses that are essential to a healthy self-image: the senses of belonging, worth, and competence.

There are three senses that are essential to a healthy self-image: the senses of *belonging, worth,* and *competence.* Subconsciously, we're always recording evidence of these three facets, seeking out whether we are part of something important, valuable to others, and capable of succeeding. Sadly, our destructive childhood recollections tend to reemerge and contradict that we belong, are worthy, and are competent unless we renew our minds with God's truth.

You Belong

The first question I will ask is: Did you fit in as a child? Were you ever called names or isolated from others? Were you made to feel unlovable or unwanted?

Purify your mind with this truth: The Father says that you *belong* to His family. Romans 8:15–16 promises, "You have not received a spirit of slavery leading to fear again, but you have received a spirit of adoption as sons by which we cry out, 'Abba! Father!' The Spirit Himself testifies with our spirit that we are children of God." You are an important and integral part of His family, the Body of Christ. You are wanted, loved, and needed.

All of heaven rejoices that you will be with the Father for all eternity (Luke 15:7, 10). Nothing can snatch you from His hand or separate you from His love (John 10:28–29; Rom. 8:38–39). This is the first thing you must understand if you wish to overcome the difficulties of your childhood.

You Are Worthy

Second, did anything occur in your youth that made you feel shame or worthlessness? Were you compared to others as you matured, never quite measuring up to others' standards? Did you feel embarrassed because of your looks, intelligence, or abilities? Did you fear that no one would ever want or respect you?

You must renew your mind with this fact: You are fully worthy to God. The Lord sacrificed *everything* to have a relationship with you, including death on the cross at Calvary (John 3:16; Rom. 8:31–32; Phil 2:5–8). Romans 5:8 confirms, "God demonstrates His own love toward us, in that while we were yet sinners, Christ died for us." Even when you were unable to do anything to please the Father, He loved you unconditionally. Therefore, He cares for you because of *who* you are, not what you *do*.

In His sight, you are "fearfully and wonderfully made," absolutely lovable and worthy.

The Lord is the only One with an unrestricted view of who you are on the inside. In His sight, you are "fearfully and wonderfully made" (Ps. 139:14), absolutely lovable and worthy. Cast aside the negative messages from your childhood and embrace this truth.

You Are Competent

Have you ever been made to feel inadequate or useless? Have you ever been prevented from pursuing a goal because you were told you could not possibly succeed? Perhaps there were some significant objectives you failed to accomplish in your life. Did others make fun of you or make you feel flawed, incapable, or hopeless?

Then it is important for you to memorize this verse and remind yourself of its promise every day: "I can do all things through Him who strengthens me" (Phil. 4:13). The Lord promises to help you succeed in whatever task He gives you, and He takes full responsibility to provide all the wisdom and power you require as you obey Him.

How does God empower you to do all the things He calls you to achieve? When you accept Jesus as your Savior, His Holy Spirit comes to dwell within you (1 Cor. 3:16). He is the One who qualifies you to complete the assignments the Lord has planned for your life (Heb. 13:20–21).

Think often about this awesome truth: "It is God who is at work in you, both to will and to work for His good pleasure" (Phil. 2:13). The omnipotent, omniscient, omnipresent Lord of creation is the One who makes you competent and enables you to do remarkable things (Mark 10:27). As Jesus said, "If you have faith the size of a mustard seed, you will say to this mountain, 'Move from here to there,' and it will move; and nothing will be impossible to you" (Matt. 17:20).

No matter what challenges or obstacles arise in life, you

can be confident of your success because He is with you. All you have to do is obey God and leave the consequences to Him. Be certain He will never steer you wrong.

MAKE THE CHOICE

Consider: Will you go through life handicapped by the past and unable to enjoy the ultimate conversation with your heavenly Father? Or will you believe what He says about you, that you belong to Him and are both worthy and competent? Those negative messages from your childhood will affect you on a daily basis unless you allow God to deal with them. Don't allow them to hinder your relationship with Him any longer. Bring your wounds and fears to the Father—talk to Him about them, listen to Him, and allow Him to heal you.

Bring your wounds and fears to the Father—talk to Him about them, listen to Him, and allow Him to heal you.

Make the choice today. As those memories from your youth surface in your life, I pray you will acknowledge they exist and confront them with truth from Scripture. Ask the Lord's forgiveness for allowing those lies to rule you, and choose to believe what He says about you. You can overcome the disparaging things others have said by embracing the fact that God Almighty wants you, loves you, and approves of you. Do not wait any longer. Accept the truth that sets you free.

||||||||||||||||||||||||||||||||||||||||||||||||||||||||||||||||||||||||||||||||||||||||||

Father, how grateful we are for Jesus, Your own loving presence with us. Thank You for the example of intimate prayer and communion that You've given us in Matthew 6. Lord God, set aside times when we can be alone with You—when we can close the door on all the distractions of life and worship You as our beloved Savior and Lord. Help us to always come before You with willing and open hearts, in humility, sincerity, and obedience.

Today I pray especially for the person who has difficulty calling You Father or who bears the scars of a difficult and painful childhood. Lord God, You know the burden that this dear soul bears daily. I pray You will deliver this individual from the hurtful experiences of youth—counteracting the lies of the enemy with the testimony of the Holy Spirit and truth from Your Word.

Please help all of Your children grasp that they belong to You, that You find them worthy, and that You make them competent. Remove all the barriers we have to knowing You and experiencing the ultimate conversation with You, Father.

Thank You for coming to set the captives free and for redeeming us from our bondage to sin. We are so grateful that You hear our prayers, Lord God. Truly, You are worthy of all of our praise.

In Jesus' precious name, I pray. Amen.

||||||||||||||||||||||||||||||||||||||||||||||||||||||||||||||||||||||||||||||||||||||||||

6

~

IN THE ASKING

What Jesus Taught Us to Request

IF GOD KNOWS WHAT YOU and I need before we ask, and if
He responds to our requests according to His will, then why
should we pray? Why should we spend time talking to the
Father if He has already decided what He wants to do?

These are questions I hear repeatedly when I'm talking to
people. Not long ago, I received an e-mail from a viewer who
was wrestling with why prayer is important for our lives. She
related that she had watched many people intercede for their
dying loved ones only to end up losing them anyway. She
recognized that God is sovereign and His plans always come
to pass. But if we cannot change His mind, what is the benefit
of taking our petitions to Him?

I imagine the reason most people pray is to ask for and
receive something from God. However, what is the Lord's
goal in interacting with us? Why does He call us into His
presence?

To answer this, we must remember what He told Israel:
"You shall love the LORD your God with all your heart and

with all your soul and with all your might" (Deut. 6:5). He wants us to love Him, and the primary reason He tells us to draw near is to deepen our intimate relationship. Jesus would tell us later that this is "the great and foremost commandment" (Matt. 22:38). The most important things to the Father are strengthening our bond with Him and enjoying profoundly satisfying and transformational fellowship.

Our first motivation in approaching God should be to know Him.

Of course, there are other reasons. We may pray for guidance, other people, comfort, or wisdom. The Lord does hear and answer our requests. But our first motivation in approaching God should be *to know Him.*

Why? Because when we spend time with the Father, we are encouraged and energized. We also mature spiritually. When we cease talking to Him, however, we begin to drift in our devotion, and that is when everything becomes confusing.

JESUS' PATTERN OF CONVERSATION

Let us think of our interaction with the Lord in terms of what Jesus taught us to request. Remember, our Savior is the perfect One to teach us how to have a meaningful conversation with the Father because He is fully God and fully man. Not only does He demonstrate how He expects us to address Him; He also shows us how to pray in a way that ministers to our spirits.

Jesus teaches you to "go into your inner room, close your door and pray to your Father" (Matt. 6:6). He wants your unhindered attention because He knows how crucial it is for you to be heard, to have your sins forgiven, and to experience the renewing of your soul.

The Savior also instructs you to seek Him privately, humbly, sincerely, and obediently, because He loves and accepts you just as you are. He doesn't want you to bear the burdens of religion; rather, He wants you to fully enjoy the blessing of a relationship with Him.

There is something in each petition that teaches us how to relate to God and meets our needs of belonging, worth, and competency.

Finally, the Lord asks you to call Him *Father*—trusting Him to be the One who loves, teaches, and provides for you faithfully.

Jesus also tells us to request certain things. As we saw in the last chapter, there is a good purpose in everything He encourages us to do. There is something in each petition that teaches us how to relate to God and meets our needs of belonging, worth, and competency.

In Matthew 6:9–13, the Savior instructs,

"Pray, then, in this way:

'Our Father who is in heaven,
Hallowed be Your name.
'Your kingdom come.
Your will be done,
On earth as it is in heaven.
'Give us this day our daily bread.
'And forgive us our debts, as we also have forgiven
our debtors.
'And do not lead us into temptation, but deliver us
from evil.
[For Yours is the kingdom and the power and the
glory forever. Amen.']"

HALLOWED BE HIS NAME

The first thing Jesus teaches us to ask is that the Lord's name be praised—that you and I recognize and revere God as sovereign and holy. He says, "Our Father who is in heaven, hallowed be Your name" (Matt. 6:9).

As we discussed in Chapter 2, we must decide in our hearts who we believe God is, because it shapes how we respond to Him and how we live. Our view of the Lord influences our attitude in approaching Him, what we communicate with Him, and whether we expect Him to answer us.

Jesus reminds us that we are talking to our Father in heaven—the Sovereign of all that exists (Ps. 103:19). He also reminds us what our goal is to be: to hallow, or bless and respect, His name. We are to bring honor and glory to the Lord with our lives. Jesus instructed, "Let your light shine before men in such a way that they may see your good works, and glorify your Father who is in heaven" (Matt. 5:16).

Jesus commands us to bring honor and glory to God not only because respect is due to Him but because doing so ministers to us as well. We have a Holy Advocate in heaven who is always fighting for us—what a marvelous privilege! We don't ever have to feel alone, hopeless, or defenseless, because our Father in heaven hears and helps us.

Understanding this caused King David to say,

> *We don't ever have to feel alone, hopeless, or defenseless, because our Father in heaven hears and helps us.*

"Yours, O LORD, is the greatness and the power and the glory and the victory and the majesty, indeed everything that is in the heavens and the earth; Yours is the dominion, O LORD, and You exalt Yourself as head over all. Both riches and honor *come* from You, and You rule over all, and in Your hand is power and might; and it lies in Your hand to make great and to strengthen everyone. Now therefore, our God, we thank You, and praise Your glorious name. But who am I and who are my people that we should be able to offer as generously as this? For all things come from You, and from Your hand we have given You." (1 Chron. 29:11–14)

HIS KINGDOM COME

Next, Jesus says, "Your kingdom come. Your will be done, on earth as it is in heaven" (Matt. 6:10). No doubt this statement would have been of interest to those listening. After all, the Jews were awaiting the Messiah, who they believed to be the mighty Warrior and King who would free them from the Roman Empire and restore the land of their inheritance to them. Roman rule was oppressive—poverty, slavery, and immorality were rampant—and the Jews looked forward to the Redeemer who would free them from all of it as the prophets had promised He would.

For example, Jeremiah wrote:

"Behold, days are coming," declares the LORD, "when I will fulfill the good word which I have spoken concerning the house of Israel and the house of Judah. In those days and at that time I will cause a righteous Branch of David to spring forth; and He shall execute justice and righteousness on the earth. In those days Judah will be saved and Jerusalem will dwell in safety; and this is the name by which she will be called: the LORD is our righteousness." For thus says the LORD, "David shall never lack a man to sit on the throne of the house of Israel." (Jer. 33:14–17)

Because of prophecies such as Jeremiah's, the Jews believed that the Messiah would come in great power to restore prosperity and well-being to the nation of Israel as David had done (Isa. 11; Jer. 23:1–7; Ezek. 34:11–31; 37; Zech. 14:1–15). And they had certain expectations of what the kingdom of God would look like.

However, as you and I realize, Jesus first had to come as the Suffering Servant (Isa. 53) who would be "pierced through for our transgressions" and by whose "scourging we are healed" (v. 6). Yes, the Lord will return one day to fulfill all of the other prophesies about Him (2 Pet. 3), but what He speaks of here is a different dominion of God than they were most likely expecting.

So when Jesus tells us to pray "Your kingdom come" (Matt. 6:10), what does He mean? The Greek word for "kingdom" here is *basileia,* and it does not necessarily indicate a geographical realm. Rather, it signifies the Lord's spiritual and eternal reign in our lives. Jesus affirms, "The Kingdom of God is within you" (Luke 17:21 TLB). It is our confession that we have chosen to allow Him to rule our hearts.

The Father wants us to let Him lead. Just like the Jews in Jesus' day, we have ideas when we come before Him, beliefs about what we want Him to do in and through us. Here, God expresses His expectation of being first in our lives— becoming the starting place of our desires, motivations, and every step we take.

This is why the Savior instructs, "Seek first His kingdom and His righteousness, and all these things will be added to you" (Matt. 6:33). Our primary pursuit should be His will and His character because then everything else falls into place.

Remember, God takes full responsibility for our needs as we obey Him.

God expresses His expectation of being first in our lives—becoming the starting place of our desires, motivations, and every step we take.

To put the Lord first in everything requires a transformation in our lives—one that does not occur overnight. The Father takes each of us through the process of *sanctification,* wherein He molds us into the image of Christ and conforms our will to His own (Rom. 8:29). It happens throughout our lives until we go to heaven. We start by praying, "Your kingdom come. Your will be done," so our spirits can begin learning this principle. We cannot pray it sincerely and continue living rebelliously.

We understand what the Lord expects of us: He wants to be first in our lives and to lead us. How does praying, "Your kingdom come. Your will be done, on earth as it is in heaven," minister to our souls and help us in the ultimate conversation?

First, Jesus tells us to pray this way because He knows how important it is for us to belong to something greater than ourselves, as we discussed in the previous chapter. Each of us is a vital and integral part of the kingdom of God—the Body of Christ needs us to do our parts. It is crucial for us to actively seek out His will.

Second, the Father has a wonderful plan for each of us. Ephesians 2:10 tells us, "We are His workmanship, created in Christ Jesus for good works, which God prepared beforehand so that we would walk in them." It is as we discover and accept the Lord's purposes for us that we find significance and profound satisfaction.

Finally, from Ecclesiastes 3:11 (TLB) we know, "God has planted eternity in the hearts of men." It is important for us to know that we are accomplishing goals that will last, that will have an effect both on earth and in heaven. When you and I obey the Father's will, we know we are impacting eternity (1 Cor. 3:11–15).

> *When you and I obey the Father's will, we know we are impacting eternity.*

OUR DAILY BREAD

The next petition Jesus instructs us to ask is "Give us this day our daily bread" (Matt. 6:11). He is not referring to a mere loaf of whole wheat or pumpernickel but to the sum of all our needs—physical, financial, spiritual, emotional, and relational. You and I are assured that our heavenly Father will take care of us.

In Matthew 6:25–26, Jesus tells us, "I say to you, do not be worried about your life, as to what you will eat or what you will drink; nor for your body, as to what you will put on. Is not life more than food, and the body more than clothing? Look at the birds of the air, that they do not sow, nor reap nor gather into barns, and yet your heavenly Father feeds them. Are you not worth much more than they?"

As believers, we can always count on God to provide for us and assume full responsibility for our needs as we obediently follow Him (Phil. 4:19). When our resources run dry and we feel as if we cannot go on any longer, the Father continues to provide for us in ways we never could have dreamed of or imagined (1 Kings 17:1–16; 19:1–8).

My grandfather taught me this principle many years ago. His face lit up as he told me the story of how God called him to proclaim the gospel and supplied all of his needs. In those days, it was usual for preachers to hold their evangelistic church meetings in tents. Granddad didn't have money to buy one. One night he walked along the road and pondered his dilemma.

Finally, my grandfather got on his knees and cried out to God: "Lord, You called me to preach, but I don't have a place to do so. I need a tent, and they cost three hundred dollars. But I don't have anything. No money. Nothing I can sell. Father, please show me what to do." It was a cry of desperation that we've all experienced. As God showed my grandfather, it is when we run out of options that He can demonstrate how mighty, wonderful, and wise He is (2 Cor. 12:9–10).

> *It is when we run out of options that God can demonstrate how mighty, wonderful, and wise He is.*

After he prayed, my grandfather got up and began walking again. When he did, he saw a house in the distance. The Holy Spirit directed him to go there. It was as if the Lord had told him, "That is where

I will provide for your needs." My grandfather wasn't sure what to make of it, but he went up to the house and knocked on the door. The smiling face that greeted him assured him he had come to the right place.

"Mr. Stanley!" exclaimed the lady at the door. "I'm so glad to see you here. I've wanted to talk to you. I have something for you." She invited him in and went to retrieve a small brown-paper sack. She handed it to him and said, "God told me to give you this."

A little stunned, he thanked her, chatted with her a while longer, and left. When he opened the sack, he found exactly enough to buy the tent he needed for the ministry—three hundred-dollar bills. Grandfather told me, "What that taught me was to always trust God, because He is faithful to provide for your needs."

This is what Jesus is saying when He calls us to acknowledge that He gives us our daily bread. The Father faithfully supplies everything we require.

> *"Always trust God, because He is faithful to provide for your needs."*

You may be thinking: *Are you sure about this? There are many things I've asked God for that He has not yet provided.* Perhaps you have asked for healing from an illness, for a job, or for the restoration of an important relationship, and you have yet to see God's movement in the situation. Will He come through for you?

Absolutely He will (Ps. 84:11).

Though He may not answer you in the way you expect, I

can assure you that what He gives is always far better than you could provide for yourself.

Jesus tells us, "What man is there among you who, when his son asks for a loaf, will give him a stone? Or if he asks for a fish, he will not give him a snake, will he? If you then, being evil, know how to give good gifts to your children, how much more will your Father who is in heaven give what is good to those who ask Him!" (Matt. 7:9–11).

What a promise! God would never furnish something that would harm you. You may not comprehend what He offers, but you can be certain that His answer to your prayers is always in your best interest (Rom. 8:28).

Jesus tells us to ask, "Give us this day our daily bread" (Matt. 6:11). Notice that He says *daily*. We are to pray not only when we have emergencies—we are to have a continual, ongoing relationship with the Lord (1 Thess. 5:17). He wants us to respect Him as the Source of everything we have and receive. As James 1:17 reminds us, "Every good thing given and every perfect gift is from above, coming down from the Father."

You can become all God created you to be only as you depend on Him.

Many people will not acknowledge this and will attempt to attain what they want with their own strength. Some expect others to help them achieve their goals. The question is: Where do *you* go for the things you require?

Jesus tells you to ask Him for your daily bread so you will understand that your hope, abilities, and sufficiency are all from Him. Mark this down: Your own strength and wisdom are inadequate for all that God has called you to accomplish. You can become all He created you to be only as you depend on Him. The first step in accepting that is thanking Him for your everyday needs.

FORGIVEN DEBTS AND PARDONED DEBTORS

The fourth request Jesus mentions is one of the most difficult but is integral. He says, "Forgive us our debts, as we also have forgiven our debtors" (Matt. 6:12). The Lord desires for us to approach Him with a clean heart.

Forgive Us Our Debts

Whether we realize it or not, whenever you and I sin, we distance ourselves from the Father. In essence, we reject His plan and presence. God is holy, and everything He commands us to do is consistent with His righteousness. So when we disobey Him, we step away from His perfect path and hinder His purifying work in our lives.

Before we know Christ, we are completely, eternally separated from the Lord because we bear the complete debt of our sins, which requires our death (Rom. 6:23). We need Jesus to be our Savior: He paid this penalty in full for us at the cross and restores our relationship with the Father so we can have everlasting life (John 3:16).

Once we trust the Lord Jesus for salvation, nothing can *eternally divide* us from God, but our sins can *impede* our relationship with Him. Yes, Jesus still lives in us—nothing can change that (John 10:28–29). But every decision we make that goes against His will, every time we choose our own preferences over His holy plan, we take a step away from the Savior.

Jesus warned against this, saying, "No one can serve two masters; for either he will hate the one and love the other, or he will be devoted to one and despise the other" (Matt. 6:24). Every time you sin, you are declaring that you want to be the lord of your life rather than God. As we know, this is inconsistent with praying "Your kingdom come. Your will be done, on earth as it is in heaven" (Matt. 6:10). For the ultimate conversation to take place, you must acknowledge that God is Lord and that He is best equipped to guide your life and lead you.

> *Every time you sin, you are declaring that you want to be the lord of your life rather than God.*

Thankfully, "if we confess our sins, He is faithful and righteous to forgive us our sins and to cleanse us from all unrighteousness" (1 John 1:9). Once we agree that we want Him to rule our lives, we can trust Him to always welcome us back.

Jesus asks you to pray for forgiveness because He does not want anything to remain between you and Him. He wants a completely free and unhindered relationship with you.

As We Forgive Our Debtors

Asking for our own forgiveness is not the only thing He instructs us to do. He says, "Forgive us our debts, *as we also have forgiven our debtors*" (Matt. 6:12, emphasis added). The Lord wants us to pardon those who have wronged us, to make sure we do not harbor any resentment, bitterness, or grudges against anyone.

That is not always so easy. It is astounding how much pain and devastation one person or a group of people can cause. Perhaps someone is coming to your mind right now. Whether the wound is fresh in your life or has been there for years, it still stings. It may even shape how you live, causing you to avoid situations or people similar to the one who injured you.

At this point you have a choice: You can nurse your anguish and become bitter, or you can turn to the Lord and allow Him to heal you and make you better. Just remember, forgiveness does not mean that we ignore the consequences of sin and disobedience or condone what a person has done. Rather, it means you give up your resentment and animosity toward his or her actions so you can be free.

I realize that this is complicated and agonizing at times. But please understand: The more difficult it is to forgive an individual, the more important it is to your spiritual, emotional, mental, and physical health that you do so. You see, unforgiveness binds you to the person who harmed you, wounding you more deeply than he or she ever could have done so alone. At some point, you must deny that individual the power to hurt you.

How do you let go and forgive?

First, you must focus on the love and compassion that Christ showed you on the cross. You have been saved solely by His sacrificial grace and goodness, not by anything you have done on your own (Eph. 2:8–9). You have been pardoned of all your sins and reconciled to the Father through His free provision of salvation—a gift you cannot earn or deserve on your own merit. You must embrace this fact fully and realize the incredible mercy shown to you in order to forgive others (Eph. 4:32).

Second, confess to God your feelings of anger, insecurity, and hurt. The Father wants to heal your wounds, help you feel safe in His care, and deliver you from any bitterness in your heart. He may reveal some sin you've been harboring or that has built up because of your unforgiveness. Be willing to admit the areas where you were wrong.

Finally, lay down your hostility and any desire you have for retaliation, recognizing that only the Lord has the authority and right to judge another. Romans 12:19 instructs, "Never take your own revenge, beloved, but leave room for the wrath of God, for it is written, 'VENGEANCE IS MINE, I WILL REPAY,' says the Lord." Again, this does not mean the person who wronged you will escape punishment. It means that you don't have to remain shackled to him or her emotionally. Instead, you trust the Father to handle the situation.

Friend, there is awesome power in forgiveness—it keeps

you from becoming bitter, resentful, and hostile. When you harbor bitterness, your fellowship with the Lord suffers. So when God reminds you of the people you need to pardon, I hope you won't ignore His voice. Bravely decide to deal with those feelings and allow the Father to set you free.

DELIVERANCE FROM EVIL

Jesus' fifth request is: "Do not lead us into temptation, but deliver us from evil" (Matt. 6:13), which may be confusing to some. After all, James 1:13 says, "Let no one say when he is tempted, 'I am be-ing tempted by God'; for God cannot be tempted by evil, and He Himself does not tempt anyone." Why would He then in-struct us to ask the Father not to guide us into situations where we would be enticed to sin?

> *Bravely decide to deal with those feelings and allow the Father to set you free.*

Let's look at the original Greek to understand what the Savior was saying. The word here for "temptation" is *peirasmos,* which can mean "to put to the test" or "to try one's character." Both carry the idea of having our virtue, faith, and integrity proved genuine through adversity.

So when we say "Do not lead us into temptation, but de-liver us from evil," we are praying that the Lord will prevent us from going the wrong direction when we face tribulations— that He will stop us from dealing with situations in ways that could harm us. In other words, "Don't allow us to be over-come by our own sinfulness when we suffer trials, or don't permit us to experience such terrible circumstances that we would fail to obey You." We are asking that He would up-hold, strengthen, and protect us when we go through dif-ficulties we cannot explain or understand so that we will not fail Him.

In this Jesus reminds us how wonderful it is to have the Lord's guidance. When we obey Him, we know that even when we are tested, He has a good purpose (Rom. 8:28). As 1 Peter 1:6–7 admonishes, "In this you greatly rejoice, even though now for a little while, if necessary, you have been distressed by various trials, so that the proof of your faith, be-ing more precious than gold which is perishable, even though tested by fire, may be found to result in praise and glory and honor at the revelation of Jesus Christ." The adversity that the Lord allows in our lives can be an awesome bridge to stronger faith and a deeper relationship with Him.

If the Father chooses to try our character, He won't give us more than we can handle but will provide the tools neces-sary so we can persevere. The apostle Paul confirms this in 1 Corinthians 10:13: "God is faithful, who will not allow you to be tempted beyond what you are able, but with the tempta-tion will provide the way of escape also, so that you will be able to endure it."

On the other hand, Jesus knows how devastating it is for us when we get ourselves into trouble. When we realize that our own bad decisions have resulted in consequences too over-whelming for us to bear, we can become furious with our-selves. If that inward anger is unresolved, it can eventually damage our whole emotional system and turn into deep, par-alyzing depression. We condemn our-selves mercilessly and reject God's grace because we feel unworthy.

Friend, the Savior does not want you to live that way. If you are often depressed, search you heart for any anger you harbor toward yourself. Confess your feelings to the Father and learn how to forgive your-self, no matter how difficult it is. Then always remember to pray, "Do not lead me into temptation, but deliver me from evil," knowing that as long as you're walking in obedience to Him, any testing that is allowed in your life will turn out for your good.

As long as you're walking in obedience to Him, any testing that is allowed in your life will turn out for your good.

HIS KINGDOM, POWER, AND GLORY FOREVER

Jesus tells us to praise God, saying, "Yours is the kingdom and the power and the glory forever. Amen" (Matt. 6:13). This declaration recognizes the Lord's supremacy and sovereignty. We give Him thanks, expressing all the ways He has been faithful in caring for us. We declare our gratefulness that He

is powerful, all-knowing, ever-present, loves us unconditionally, and is always willing to lead us. And we give Him all the
honor and glory for our successes.

Though that is His due as our God, it is also vital to our
well-being. Praise reminds us of our dependence upon Him
and that no matter what issue we're facing, He is able to lead
us to triumph. In fact, the Father already knows everything
we need, and He is already at work delivering us. If we respond with faith and trust in Him, our obstacles will result in
our blessing and edification.

Therefore, like the apostle Paul, we can and should declare: "Thanks be to God, who gives us the victory through
our Lord Jesus Christ!" (1 Cor. 15:57).

ALONE WITH THE FATHER

From beginning to end, the Savior's pattern of conversation
is centered on God: His authority, holiness, power, wisdom,
purpose, provision, forgiveness, and goodness. When we focus on the Lord and meditate on His ways, we begin to love
Him, listen to Him, and sense His presence, and He speaks to
us in awesome ways.

As you follow Jesus' pattern in prayer, you will grow in
your intimate relationship with God and experience the ultimate conversation. It may feel strange at first. I promise, if you
do so, soon enough you will yearn for the Father's presence.
There are things that you cannot tell anyone but God and is-

sues in your life that only He understands fully. Your heart will cry out for the privilege of spending time with the One who knows you perfectly—including your fears and failings—and loves you just the same.

Therefore, get alone with Him as the Savior instructed: "When you pray, go into your inner room, close your door and pray to your Father" (Matt. 6:6). Do you have an inner room or "prayer closet" where you can be with God and experience His presence? Do you have a place to go and meet with the Lord undisturbed?

When I was a teenager, the only place in our small house where I could be un-interrupted was the bathroom. There were many times when I would go there, stretch out on the floor, and talk to the Lord. He spoke powerfully to me during those quiet hours. He didn't care that I was in the bathroom, just that my heart was open to His voice.

As you follow Jesus' pattern in prayer, you will grow in your intimate relationship with God and experience the ultimate conversation.

It doesn't matter where your prayer closet or inner room is, only that you show up. God is always far more interested in your spiritual growth than where you meet with Him. Find a place where you and He can communicate daily without disruption.

Are you willing? I hope so. I pray that you will follow the Savior's pattern of conversation and see how deeply fulfilling your fellowship with the Father can be.

Father, we love You and thank You for giving us this pattern of conversation as a guide to genuine, exciting, satisfying communion with You. I pray that each of us will apply it to our hearts and commit ourselves to knowing You in more profound and intimate ways—especially those who have been repeating this prayer throughout the years but never felt any closer to You. May each of us experience the powerful privilege of walking in Your presence moment by moment each day.

Lord, I pray specifically for this reader: if this individual does not have a prayer closet yet, please identify an inner room to meet together. Draw this dear person into complete, unhindered fellowship so that he or she may seek You privately, humbly, sincerely, and obediently, fully experiencing Your unconditional love. Help this soul cast off the burdens of religion and realize the blessing of a relationship with You as the beloved Father. May this reader acknowledge You as Defender, allow You to lead as Sovereign God, seek You as Provider of every need, wholeheartedly accept Your pardon, freely forgive others, and stay in the center of Your will.

For Yours is the kingdom and the power and the glory forever, and we praise You joyfully. In the matchless name of Jesus our Lord and Savior. Amen.

7

OUR HELPER IN PRAYER

The Holy Spirit as Our Ambassador

IT CAN BEGIN AS A soft tugging in your spirit or a twinge in your heart. Your internal antenna goes up. You are suddenly aware that you should be paying attention to something important.

Several years ago during a photographic trip, my group had been traveling up a trail for almost three hours, and I began to have a funny feeling that we were going in the wrong direction. I asked the guide about it, and he assured me that everything was fine. Not wanting to be presumptuous, I kept walking.

After a few minutes, I noticed that my sense of uneasiness persisted; in fact, it was growing stronger. I pulled out my compass and looked at the map. Sure enough, we were headed away from our intended destination.

It took us close to an hour and a half to return to where we had taken the incorrect turn off the trail. Sadly, this meant that by the time we got to the site, our window for taking photographs was cut short.

The event helped me to realize two valuable lessons. First, when we sense an internal witness encouraging us to take a certain course of action, we should listen. Second, when you and I choose people to guide us, we must be certain they know the path ahead better than we do.

Consider: Have you ever felt something alerting you to pay attention, or pulling you in a particular direction? Perhaps you were listening to a sermon and you sensed God telling you to follow Him in obedience. Or maybe you walked into a restaurant and were filled with dread, as if you should leave quickly.

If you are a believer, then most likely these feelings were the prompting of the Holy Spirit, who always guides you to understand and accept the Father's will. He is the One speaking to your heart, warning you about danger and encouraging you to submit to God's purposes.

The Holy Spirit is a trustworthy guide who will never lead us astray and knows the path ahead much better than we do.

Unlike the fellow who accompanied us on that photographic trip, the Holy Spirit is a trustworthy guide who will never lead us astray and knows the path ahead much better than we do. Apart from Him, you and I cannot live a godly life. Galatians 5:16 instructs, "Walk by the Spirit, and you will not carry out the desire of the flesh." This is because the Holy Spirit empowers us to resist sin and obey God, helps us to understand Scripture, and enables us to achieve fellowship with the

Lord. He will never advise us to do anything that contradicts Scripture.

In fact, of all the professors I had in college, none ever matched the personal instruction I have received from God through the Holy Spirit. In John 14:26, Jesus promised the disciples: "The Helper, the Holy Spirit, whom the Father will send in My name, He will teach you all things, and bring to your remembrance all that I said to you." I remember how powerfully the Lord communicated this to me one night on my knees when I was in graduate school.

After graduating from the University of Richmond, I went to Southwestern Baptist Theological Seminary in Fort Worth, Texas. I was about halfway through the three-year program and I was beginning to think about my future. It was one of those nights when I longed to pick up the phone and call the father I never knew and tell him what I was thinking. Little did I know how God used that void in my heart for a father over and over again to draw me to Himself.

That night as I knelt to pray, I had a very strong sense of the Lord's presence. I did not hear His voice audibly, but His message to me could not have been clearer. He said, "Whatever you accomplish in life will not depend upon your education, your talent, or your skill. I have a plan for you, but you will only accomplish it on your knees in complete surrender to Me."

I have never forgotten that night. And throughout my life I have started and ended my days on my knees before God to talk to Him and to listen to what else He has to say.

THE HELPER'S ROLE

What the Father communicated to me that night was the same message that we read in Zechariah 4:6, "'Not by might nor by power, but by My Spirit,' says the LORD of hosts." The Holy Spirit's presence with us is especially important as we engage in the ultimate conversation because He is God's own Spirit. He teaches us the Father's will, how to listen to Him, how to discern His truth, and how to have an intimate relationship with Him. He also trains and empowers us to fulfill God's plans for our lives with the "wisdom from above" (James 3:17).

The apostle Paul explains,

EYE HAS NOT SEEN AND EAR HAS NOT HEARD, AND *which* HAVE NOT ENTERED THE HEART OF MAN, ALL THAT GOD HAS PREPARED FOR THOSE WHO LOVE HIM.

For to us God revealed *them* through the Spirit; for the Spirit searches all things, even the depths of God. For who among men knows the *thoughts* of a man except the spirit of the man which is in him? Even so the *thoughts* of God no one knows except the Spirit of God. Now we have received, not the spirit of the world, but the Spirit who is from God, so that we may know the things freely given to us by God, which things we also speak, not in words taught by human wisdom, but in those taught by the Spirit, combining spiritual *thoughts* with spiritual *words*. . . .

For WHO HAS KNOWN THE MIND OF THE LORD, THAT
HE WILL INSTRUCT HIM? But we have the mind of Christ.
(1 Cor. 2:9–13, 16)

In other words, because the Holy Spirit lives within you, you have the Lord's constant presence and guidance (1 Cor. 3:16; 6:19; 2 Cor. 6:16). If you ever struggle with knowing what to say to the Father, or wish you had a better vocabulary to address Him, let not your heart be troubled. You don't have to wonder whether God understands what you mean or if you have asked for the wrong thing. He has given you the Helper, who is always with you and helps you pray. The question is whether or not you'll listen to Him.

Perhaps you are wondering: *Who is the Holy Spirit? Why should I trust Him?* Along with the Father and Jesus the Son, the Holy Spirit is part of the Godhead. Does this mean there are three deities? No, there is only one God whom we serve and worship (Deut. 6:4; 1 Cor. 8:6). But when we look at Scripture, we see that the Lord expresses Himself as three Persons, also known as the Trinity (Matt. 28:19; Luke 3:22; Acts 2:32–33; 7:55; 2 Cor. 13:14; 1 Pet. 1:2). He reveals Himself to us as the Father (Matt. 6:9; Rom. 8:14–15; Eph. 4:6), as our Savior Jesus (Acts 13:23; Phil. 3:20; 2 Tim. 1:10; Titus 3:5–7), and as the Holy Spirit (John 14:26; 20:22; 1 Cor. 6:19).

> *Because the Holy Spirit lives within you, you have the Lord's constant presence and guidance.*

The Holy Spirit has the same attributes as the other members of the Godhead—He is absolutely holy, unchanging, omnipotent, omniscient, and omnipresent. He is not an impersonal force; rather, He is a Person who loves you unconditionally.

On the night before His crucifixion, after the Last Supper, the Savior explained the Holy Spirit's mission and purpose:

I will ask the Father, and He will give you another Helper, that He may be with you forever; that is the Spirit of truth, whom the world cannot receive, because it does not see Him or know Him, but you know Him because He abides with you and will be in you. . . . The Helper, the Holy Spirit, whom the Father will send in My name, He will teach you all things, and bring to your remembrance all that I said to you. (John 14:16–17, 26)

It is important for us to understand that Jesus was sending the Holy Spirit to be with us *permanently*. However, this was not the first time that Scripture had mentioned the Spirit. From the beginning in Genesis, we can see His activity: "The earth was formless and void, and darkness was over the surface of the deep, and the Spirit of God was moving over the surface of the waters" (1:2). The Holy Spirit was at hand, but only a hundred or so people in the Old Testament had the privilege of His presence (Ex. 31:3; Num. 11:25–26; 1 Sam. 11:6), and usually, He did not remain with them (1 Sam. 15:16).

God understood that for us to truly experience the ultimate conversation with Him, He would always need to be present with us. He said, "I will give you a new heart and put a new spirit within you; and I will remove the heart of stone from your flesh and give you a heart of flesh. I will put My Spirit within you and cause you to walk in My statutes, and you will be careful to observe My ordinances" (Ezek. 36:26–27). What an honor to always have Him with us! He is our ever-present refuge and strength in every situation and circumstance (Ps. 46:1).

> *God understood that for us to truly experience the ultimate conversation with Him, He would always need to be present with us.*

How does the Holy Spirit help us?

- He draws us to the cross, revealing our need for forgiveness and demonstrating how to have faith in Christ as our Savior (John 15:26).
- He gives us assurance of our salvation (John 14:20) and "testifies with our spirit that we are children of God" (Rom. 8:16).
- He guarantees our redemption—making us eternally secure—by sealing us in Christ (Eph. 1:13; 4:30).
- He guides our steps and helps us discover the Lord's plans for us (Mark 1:12; John 16:13–15; Rom. 8:14).
- He walks with us every step of the way in becoming the children of God, helping and com-

forting us as we follow the Father (John 14:16–17, 26; Rom. 8:14–16).

- He teaches us the truth by helping us understand and apply Scripture (John 16:13; 1 Cor. 2:9–13, 16).

- He reminds us of what we have learned, bringing verses and biblical principles to mind so we can stay in the center of God's will (John 14:26).

- He convicts us of our sins so we can repent of them, and removes any hindrances to our intimate relationship with the Lord (John 16:8–11).

- He empowers us to accomplish God's will (Zech. 4:6; Acts 10:44; 1 Thess. 1:5).

- He helps us share the Good News of salvation with others (John 15:27; Acts 1:7–8).

- He equips us to minister to others and gives us spiritual gifts so we can serve the Body of Christ (1 Cor. 12:4–8; Eph. 4:11–12).

- He produces eternal fruit in and through us (Gal. 5:22–23).

- He helps us pray, interceding for us "with groaning too deep for words" (Rom. 8:26–27).

- He searches us, seeking out the wounds that must be healed and the sinful habits that must be expelled (Ps. 139:23–24; Heb. 9:14; Titus 3:5).

- He makes us into new people, transforming us into the likeness of Jesus Christ (Ezek. 36:26–27; Rom. 8:27–29; 2 Cor. 3:17–18).

HIS STRENGTH IN OUR WEAKNESS

The Father has given us an awesome gift by sending the Helper to dwell in us. He is like an ambassador who unswervingly represents the policies of His homeland and also serves the host nation by translating its messages into the appropriate language. The Holy Spirit faithfully conveys to us the Father's will in a way we understand, and He represents us before God in a manner worthy of His righteous name.

The apostle Paul wrote, "The Spirit also helps our weakness; for we do not know how to pray as we should, but the Spirit Himself intercedes for us with groanings too deep for words; and He who searches the hearts knows what the mind of the Spirit is, because He intercedes for the saints according to the will of God" (Rom. 8:26–27).

"The Spirit . . . intercedes for the saints according to the will of God" (Rom. 8:27).

What is our weakness in the ultimate conversation? At times we do not know how to express the full depth of our desires or feelings; nor do we realize what we need. Sometimes we are so exhausted—in spirit, mind, and body—that we can hardly muster the energy to open our mouths. There are instances when discouragement has taken such a strong hold of our hearts that we cannot imagine a way out of our painful circumstances, and all we can ask is for the Father to help us.

Perhaps this is where Paul found himself. In 2 Corinthians 1:8–9, he confesses, "We do not want you to be unaware, brethren, of our affliction which came to us in Asia, that we were burdened excessively, beyond our strength, so that we despaired even of life; indeed, we had the sentence of death within ourselves so that we would not trust in ourselves, but in God who raises the dead."

With the lashes, imprisonments, and dangers Paul experienced, it is not surprising that he would feel this way (2 Cor. 11:23–29). The apostle faced terrible difficulties during his missionary journeys, including being stoned almost to death at Lystra (Acts 14:19), at the center of a riot in Ephesus (Acts 19:23–41), and having to leave behind his beloved churches in order to suffer in Jerusalem (Acts 20:17–24). In constant peril, separated from his loved ones, threatened on every side, and buffeted by innumerable trials, he had good reason to be disheartened.

Have you ever felt this way? Have you ever been so encumbered by troubles that hopelessness takes over? You struggle to find a reason to keep fighting, but you are so tired and overwhelmed that you just want to give up?

Despite all his adversity, the apostle Paul continued to trust God, and you should, too. Be assured that the Helper sees the depths of your difficulties. He translates your feelings more accurately than you could articulate them yourself. And He comforts you with the knowledge that He understands what you need.

You should never fear whether God will acknowledge the cries of your heart because His Holy Spirit transforms your petitions into acceptable and pleasing sacrifices (Rev. 5:8; 8:3–4). Even when you think you're failing in your prayers, the Holy Spirit ensures that you are heard. He also guarantees that your tribulations are not in vain but will build you up in the faith if you respond to Him in obedience.

OBEYING HIS PROMPTINGS

Do not miss that: *Responding to the Holy Spirit in obedience is key.* This part of the conversation is yours—your willing submission to what the Holy Spirit tells you. He teaches you how to listen to the Father, communicating the truth in a way you can receive. According to your spiritual maturity, He shows you how to apply biblical principles to your life. Your part is to obey Him, and as you do, He strengthens you (1 Pet. 5:10).

Responding to the Holy Spirit in obedience is key.

It is not a mystery how Paul was able to endure such heartache and persecution. The apostle had learned to listen closely to the Holy Spirit and had drawn the encouragement he needed from His constant presence. How did Paul do so? He learned to walk by the Spirit. The apostle explained:

I say, walk by the Spirit, and you will not carry out the desire of the flesh. For the flesh sets its desire against the

Spirit, and the Spirit against the flesh; for these are in opposition to one another, so that you may not do the things that you please. But if you are led by the Spirit, you are not under the Law. Now the deeds of the flesh are evident, which are: immorality, impurity, sensuality, idolatry, sorcery, enmities, strife, jealousy, outbursts of anger, disputes, dissensions, factions, envying, drunkenness, carousing, and things like these, of which I forewarn you, just as I have forewarned you, that those who practice such things will not inherit the kingdom of God. But the fruit of the Spirit is love, joy, peace, patience, kindness, goodness, faithfulness, gentleness, self-control; against such things there is no law. Now those who belong to Christ Jesus have crucified the flesh with its passions and desires. If we live by the Spirit, let us also walk by the Spirit. (Gal. 5:16–25)

Paul learned to deal with his troubles in God's way, rather than the ways of the world. When we experience difficulty, our human nature tries to express or quench it in ungodly ways: through possessions, addictions, or immorality. However, Paul realized that if he listened to the Spirit—handling his adversity as Christ would—he would be set free from the worries and discouragements of this life.

You can be, too. You can crucify the desires of the flesh—those things that are subtly destroying you and causing you heartache day by day—by learning to walk in the Spirit.

Perhaps you are wondering what the phrase "walk in the Spirit" means for your life. How do you do that? How can you live each moment in dependence on the Holy Spirit, sensitive to His voice, and obedient to Him?

To walk in the Spirit means obeying His initial promptings. You do so by going through each day aware of the Holy Spirit's presence with you. You submit to Him as you feel Him pulling you in a certain direction or tugging at your heart to take a particular course of action, even if you don't quite understand why He is doing so.

For example, you may be convicted to drop a conversation, turn away quickly from a television program, or leave a place that is questionable. Whatever it is, do so immediately—the Spirit is warning you about a temptation to sin that you may be unable to resist unless you obey Him instantly.

To walk in the Spirit means obeying His initial promptings— submitting to Him as you feel Him pulling you in a certain direction.

Perhaps there is someone who comes to your mind during the day. You know he or she has been going through a difficult time and could use some support. Call or write to that person. The Spirit will give you the right words to encourage him or her. He wants to minister to that person through you and is sure to bless you as you do so.

The Holy Spirit may guide you to pursue a route or a risk that you never imagined you would take. The wisest thing to do is to submit to His plan, regardless of whether it makes sense to you. The Spirit of the living God knows all things, including the future, and His direction is always for your benefit.

A LIVING CONVERSATION

This is the way the ultimate conversation becomes real in your life—you obey the initial promptings of the Holy Spirit. And as you do, the voice of God becomes stronger and more prevalent in your life. Eventually, you begin to see spiritual realities that only a person who is in constant communion with the Father can perceive (Ps. 25:14).

> *As you obey the promptings of the Spirit, you will begin to see spiritual realities that only a person who is in constant communion with the Father can perceive.*

Elisha was just such an individual (2 Kings 6:8–19). When the Arameans gathered against Israel and surrounded the city of Dothan, the prophet was unafraid and unmoved. His servant, on the other hand, saw that multitude of soldiers, horses, and chariots and was terrified. He cried out, "Alas, my master! What shall we do?" (v. 15).

Elisha remained calm. "Do not fear," he replied. " 'Those who are with us are more than those who are with them.' Then Elisha prayed and said, 'O Lord, I pray, open his eyes that he may see.' And the LORD opened the servant's eyes and he saw; and behold, the mountain was full of horses and chariots of fire all around Elisha" (vv. 16–17).

While the servant saw that the enemy had encamped around the city, Elisha perceived the greater spiritual reality: that God was fighting the battle for them. The prophet remained confident and secure. Likewise, the more you obey the Spirit and the closer you grow to the Father, the stronger your faith and assurance. You can see this truth demonstrated throughout Scripture:

- "Though I walk through the valley of the shadow of death, I fear no evil, for You are with me, Your rod and Your staff, they comfort me." (Ps. 23:4)
- "The LORD is my light and my salvation; whom shall I fear? The LORD is the defense of my life; whom shall I dread? . . . Though a host encamp against me, my heart will not fear; though war arise against me, in spite of this I shall be confident." (Ps. 27:1, 3)
- "God is our refuge and strength, a very present help in trouble. Therefore we will not fear, though the earth should change and though the mountains slip into the heart of the sea." (Ps. 46:1–2)
- "He who dwells in the shelter of the Most High will abide in the shadow of the Almighty. I will say to the LORD, 'My refuge and my fortress, my

God, in whom I trust!' For it is He who deliv-
ers you from the snare of the trapper and from
the deadly pestilence. He will cover you with His
pinions, and under His wings you may seek refuge; His faithfulness is a shield and bulwark. You
will not be afraid of the terror by night, or of the
arrow that flies by day." (Ps. 91:1–5)

- "How blessed is the man who fears the LORD . . .
For he will never be shaken; The righteous will
be remembered forever. He will not fear evil tid-
ings; his heart is steadfast, trusting in the LORD."
(Ps. 112:1, 6–7)

- "Blessed is the man who trusts in the LORD and
whose trust is the LORD. For he will be like a tree
planted by the water, that extends its roots by a
stream and will not fear when the heat comes; but
its leaves will be green, and it will not be anxious in a year of drought nor cease to yield fruit."
(Jer. 17:7–8)

This does not mean that if you walk by the Spirit, you'll
never be afraid. Nor does it signify that you will automatically
see the Lord's angelic host, as Elisha and his servant did.

The point is, when you engage in the ultimate conversation
with the Father in a real and living way, you begin to know and
understand things that are apparent only to those who understand the deep truths of the Holy Spirit (1 Cor. 2:6–16). As God
Himself says, "Call to me and I will answer you and tell you

great and unsearchable things you do not know" (Jer. 33:3 NIV). You experience more of the Father's faultless character and grow more confident in His provision for you.

Therefore, I challenge you to begin each morning with a prayer that goes something like this: "Father, I want You to guide me and lead me today. Speak to my heart. Make me sensitive to Your promptings and to what is happening around me in the lives of those I meet. Fill me with Your supernatural joy, and use me today for Your purposes. I surrender fully to You."

If you yield to the Holy Spirit and depend on His ability rather than your own, He will enable you not only to live a life that is pleasing to Christ but also to experience God in ways you never thought possible.

Father, how grateful we are for Your awesome love and for the wonderful gift of Your Holy Spirit. You have done so much in preparation for our daily life, Lord. We can wake up each day knowing You are with us and live with perfect assurance of Your favor.

Father, our desire is to walk with Your Spirit moment by moment. Teach us how to respond to Your promptings immediately. Show us how to rely more on You every hour of each day so we can grow deeper in our relationships with You.

(continued on next page)

Father, I pray specifically for this reader. Let this dear soul experience the transformational work of the Holy Spirit in a radical way. I know this person wants Your best, Lord, so do not allow this individual to ignore Your warnings or admonishments. Rather, help this reader always respond to You in obedience. I pray Your Holy Spirit will seal this message into this person's heart—making the ultimate conversation real and living communion with You.

Thank You for the wonderful privilege of Your presence today and every day. In Jesus' name, I pray. Amen.

8

HOW GOD USES SILENCE

His Message in the Stillness

WE HAVE BEEN EXAMINING THE ongoing, living conversation that you and I can have with God, and we know that not only does He speak; He also gives us the Holy Spirit as His constant agent of communication within us. However, if you have been experiencing the Lord's silence, you may be a little frustrated by now. What do we do when it looks like the Father has stopped interacting with us?

Please understand, I'm not talking about people who think the Lord has *never* addressed them. God *is* communicating with them, but their ears may not be trained to hear His call.

No, I am discussing what happens when people who know how to listen to the Father no longer perceive the sound of His voice. Though they are seeking His presence and direction, He seems absent from their situations, as if He's stopped speaking to them altogether.

Perhaps you're going through such a time right now. For whatever reason, God appears to be giving you the silent treatment. Maybe you've asked for guidance and He does not answer. It could be that He has not provided for a pressing need in your life, and you feel as if He is distant, uninterested in your difficult circumstances.

He will use the silence to develop your intimacy with Him and mature you spiritually if you continue to seek Him.

The truth is, our heavenly Father is sometimes quiet, and when we're hurting, His silence can be particularly perplexing to us. We may become confused and disheartened, wondering if the Lord has rejected us. Be assured that God still loves you and has a good purpose for His silence. He will use it to develop your intimacy with Him and mature you spiritually if you continue to seek Him.

FOUR HUNDRED YEARS OF PREPARATION

As an example, we can look at one of the most significant periods of God's silence in history. As we saw from our study of Nehemiah in Chapters 2 and 3, after the seventy years of captivity in Babylon, the Lord allowed the Jews to return to Jerusalem to rebuild the holy temple and the city's protective walls. After that, there was revival in Israel. The people were wholeheartedly committed to obeying God and signed a document as a guarantee that they would submit to His commands (Neh. 8–10).

Unfortunately, their renewed desire to honor and serve the Father did not last long. Soon enough, the priests began failing in their service to the Lord, offering Him defiled sacrifices and allowing immorality to run rampant. God rebuked them through the prophet Malachi, saying, "'You have turned aside from the way; you have caused many to stumble by the instruction. . . . So I also have made you despised and abased before all the people'" (2:8–9).

Like the generations before them, the Israelites fell into their old patterns of disobedience, engaging in ungodly practices and oppressing the helpless (3:5), marrying people who served other deities (2:11; see also Deut. 7:1–6), failing to give their tithes and offerings (3:7–9), and dishonoring His name (3:13–15). They had been here many times and had been punished for their behavior.

However, this time the Lord treated them somewhat differently. After admonishing the people through the prophet Malachi, He grew quiet. No other prophet, priest, judge, or king arose to make sure they stayed on track. God simply stopped speaking and didn't say anything else—for four hundred years!

Had the people of Israel sinned so badly that the Lord gave up trying to correct their behavior? Did He get so angry with them that He just walked away, abandoning them to their destructive habits? *Absolutely not.*

Did this lack of communication mean God had stopped working on their behalf? Had He forgotten the covenants He made with their forefathers (Gen. 12:1–3; 15; 2 Sam. 7:8–16)? *No way.*

Rather, the Lord was preparing Israel for the most important event in her history—the coming of the Messiah. During those four quiet centuries, God was actively setting the world stage for the Savior to redeem mankind. And what He accomplished was astounding.

First, in Malachi's time, there was no common language by which to spread the gospel worldwide. Beginning in 336 B.C., Greek conqueror Alexander the Great of Macedon began defeating one empire after another, including the majority of Asia Minor, Phoenicia, Egypt, Mesopotamia, Persia, and even some parts of India. Seeking to unite such disparate nations, Alexander spread Greek culture and language (a process known as Hellenization) throughout the territories, making it the standard of commerce, science, and philosophy. Therefore, by the time Jesus was born, communicating the gospel was much easier, as there was a common vernacular.

In fact, Hellenization was so prevalent throughout the world that the Jews even translated the Hebrew Bible into the *Septuagint*—the Greek equivalent of the Old Testament. This second development made Scripture much more accessible, which was beneficial in spreading the Good News of salvation.

Although Alexander's efforts made Greek the common language, it was still dangerous to travel between nations. However, with the rise of the Roman Empire came an immense improvement of roads and a time of relative peace known as the *Pax Romana*. This third advance made it easier for early evangelists to "make disciples of all the nations" (Matt. 28:19) and to be Jesus' "witnesses . . . even to the remotest part of the earth" (Acts 1:8).

Finally, there were countless Jews scattered throughout the Roman provinces who had established synagogues—places to assemble for prayer and the study of Scripture. They gave missionaries centers from which to reach Jewish communities with the gospel and from which to preach throughout the known world.

---

c. 538 B.C.	Cyrus decrees that Jews can return to Jerusalem
c. 537 B.C.	Jews begin returning to Jerusalem to rebuild the temple
c. 445 B.C.	God works through Nehemiah to restore Jerusalem's walls
c. 430 B.C.	Malachi prophesies against immorality in Israel
c. 336–323 B.C.	Greek Empire emerges through Alexander the Great's conquests
c. 197–146 B.C.	Greek city-states fall one by one to Roman expansion
c. 63 B.C.	Pompey of Rome conquers Judea
c. 1 B.C.	The angel Gabriel tells Zacharias of his son John, forerunner to the Messiah: the first prophecy in four centuries

---

By the time Jesus rose from the dead, the known world had been prepared with important communication innovations to receive the gospel. Yes, God was silent, but He was not unengaged. He had not forgotten or abandoned His people. Rather, He was working to help Israel with its sin problem.

Throughout history, the Israelites had proved unequivocally that no matter how good our intentions, we humans can never handle the burden of our transgressions alone. The apostle Paul explains, "I joyfully concur with the law of God in the inner man, but I see a different law in the members of my body, waging war against the law of my mind and making me a prisoner of the law of sin which is in my members. Wretched man that I am! Who will set me free from the body of this death?" (Rom. 7:22–24).

In other words, no matter how much we love the Father, the sinful nature within us will always lead us to rebel against Him. As Paul says, we don't want to sin, but we do so anyway (Rom. 7:14–17). So you and I need a Savior who can break the hold of sin within us and set us free.

Paul tells us where that liberty is found: "Thanks be to God through Jesus Christ our Lord! . . . Therefore there is now no condemnation for those who are in Christ Jesus. For the law of the Spirit of life in Christ Jesus has set you free from the law of sin and of death" (Rom. 7:25; 8:1–2).

Rather than ignoring the Israelites through His silence, God was setting them free from sin once and for all through the Messiah—an awesome blessing we can embrace as well.

SIX WAYS GOD USES SILENCE

I say all of this to assure you that if God is giving you the silent treatment, you have no need to fear. He is not angry with you, nor has He stopped loving you. He continues to work on your behalf.

However, I would say this: *If the Father is quiet, then most likely there is something significant He desires to teach you, and He wants you to listen.* Therefore, we are going to look at six reasons why the Lord may be inaudible at the moment.

> *If the Father is quiet, then most likely there is something significant He desires to teach you, and He wants you to listen.*

1. Getting Our Attention

There are times when we get so caught up in our own activities, needs, and relationships that we fail to focus on the Father or spend time with Him. We pursue our goals in our own strength, becoming so busy we don't even think about Him. At other times, He's not saying what we want to hear, so we shut Him out of our lives.

Either way, God will use the silence to get our attention. Eventually, when our souls become starved for His presence, we must retrace our steps to see where we've walked away from Him.

Although the prophet Elijah was a godly man who loved and served God faithfully, there was a point in his ministry when he took his eyes off the Lord and fixed them on his circumstances. The wicked Jezebel threatened to execute him, which terrified him (1 Kings 19:1–2). He fled into the wilderness, eighty to ninety miles from Jezebel's home in Samaria and far out of her reach. He was exhausted and wanted to die, but the angel of the Lord fed him. Strengthened by the nourishment, he traveled another forty days to Mount Horeb— even farther from the evil queen.

Finally, the Lord spoke to him: "What are you doing here, Elijah?" (1 Kings 19:9). Elijah, knowing how far he was from his assigned field of ministry, offered this explanation: "I have been very zealous for the LORD, the God of hosts; for the sons of Israel have forsaken Your covenant, torn down Your altars and killed Your prophets with the sword. And I alone am left; and they seek my life, to take it away" (1 Kings 19:10). The prophet was obviously afraid, tired, and focused on Jezebel's threats. So the Father took profound steps to readjust his mind. God said:

"Go forth and stand on the mountain before the LORD." And behold, the LORD was passing by! And a great and strong wind was rending the mountains and breaking in pieces the rocks before the LORD; but the LORD was not in the wind. And after the wind an earthquake, but the LORD was not in the earthquake. After the earthquake a fire, but the LORD was not in the fire; and after the fire a sound of a gentle blowing. When Elijah heard it, he wrapped his face in his mantle and went out and stood in the entrance of the cave. (1 Kings 19:11–13)

Through the destructive wind, earthquake, and fire, the Father got the prophet Elijah's attention. After all, the God who could rend the mountains could surely take care of that wicked queen. Elijah had nothing to fear as long as he trusted the Lord.

Whenever you get your focus off the Father, He may send some powerful silence to change your perspective. Listen to Him.

Likewise, whenever you get your focus off the Father, He may send some powerful silence to change your perspective. Listen to Him.

2. Preparing Us to Obey Him

Sometimes God is silent when we ask Him about a significant decision or trial because He knows His distance causes us to seek Him more passionately. His desire is for us to reach a point where we are ready and eager to obey Him—when we acknowledge that He is Lord and knows what is best for us. After our time of intensely seeking His direction, He rewards our request for His will and gives us the guidance we've asked Him to provide.

In such cases, no matter how difficult the challenges or choices ahead of you, remember David's testimony: "I would have despaired unless I had believed that I would see the goodness of the LORD in the land of the living. Wait for the LORD; be strong and let your heart take courage; yes, wait for the LORD" (Ps. 27:13–14).

You will hear God's voice again and see His mighty work in your life. So be patient, acknowledge His rightful place in your life, and keep listening.

3. Revealing Our Sin

The Father wants to make us aware of sin in our lives—not out of spite or meanness but out of loving-kindness and compassion. You see, our transgressions are terribly destructive. They hurt our fellowship with Him, damage our relationships with others, and wound us. Sin can devastate us—in body, mind, and spirit—leaving us broken and without hope. So God will wait to speak with us until we are willing to repent, turn away from these injurious behaviors, and seek His life-giving ways.

David confessed,

When I kept silent about my sin, my body wasted away through my groaning all day long. For day and night Your hand was heavy upon me; my vitality was drained away *as* with the fever heat of summer. I acknowledged my sin to You, and my iniquity I did not hide; I said, "I will confess my transgressions to the LORD"; and You forgave the guilt of my sin. Therefore, let everyone who is godly pray to You in a time when You may be found. . . . Many are the sorrows of the wicked, but he who trusts in the LORD, loving-kindness shall surround him. (Ps. 32:3–6, 9)

Whenever the Lord God is quiet, I encourage you to examine your heart and make sure you are not harboring any sin. Do you feel the same way David did? Is there something bothering you that you cannot identify? Are you bearing some heaviness in your spirit that is depleting all your energy? Does it seem as if your relationships and plans are going awry?

If so, then ask God to identify your iniquity and set you free from it. Then, like David, you can say, "How blessed is he whose transgression is forgiven, whose sin is covered!" (Ps. 32:1).

4. Growing Our Trust in Him

Sometimes we desire to honor God as our sovereign Lord, but we're afraid to trust Him. So the Father must stretch our faith. By choosing to be silent, He sometimes tests how deeply we believe in Him and how tenaciously we will cling to His promises. This is not for His benefit; He knows exactly how strong our trust is. Rather, He does so to reveal areas where we need to grow.

I faced a time like this when I was in my teens. By the age of fourteen, I knew God was calling me to be a pastor, but I could not see any possibility of going to university and seminary because my family did not have the funds to send me. I worked after school and on weekends delivering newspapers, and I had a side job washing cars at a local service station. I made about eighteen dollars a week, which was enough to buy my school lunches, clothes, and shoes, and also help my mother with some of the household expenses. But it was far from what was required for college.

By choosing to be silent, God sometimes tests how deeply we believe in Him and how tenaciously we will cling to His promises.

Mother always encouraged me to pray about all my needs. She and I would kneel together and ask the Father to make a way for me to be trained so I could serve Him as a pastor. After we prayed, Mother would say, "You know, the Lord's going to provide. I don't know how, but if He's called you to preach, He will give you everything you require."

By the time I turned seventeen and began preparing for my high school graduation, I still had no answers about how He would provide for me. In faith, I applied to the history program at the University of Richmond and was accepted. As the months passed, I wondered how the Lord would pull everything together.

Because of the Father's silence, my trust in Him was put to the test. Would I trust Him to take care of me, or would I give up? Did I truly believe the promise of Philippians 4:19, "My God will supply all your needs according to His riches in glory in Christ Jesus"? Was my faith real, or was it just words?

Thankfully, the Father was right on time, as He always is.

One night I was talking to my friend Julian when the pastor of Moffett Memorial Baptist Church walked by and stopped to visit with us. Julian did not waste a bit of time but spoke right up. He said, "Mr. Hammock, Charles believes the Lord has called him to preach, but he doesn't have any money to go to school. Can you do anything for him?"

Mr. Hammock thought a minute and then replied with a smile, "I think I can help with that." God worked through him in a powerful way. Mr. Hammock helped me get not only a four-year scholarship but also some money for living expenses. Seven years later, in 1956, I was ordained as a pastor at his church, Moffett Memorial Baptist.

The principles the Lord taught me through His silence were powerful: He acts on behalf of those who wait for Him, and He takes full responsibility for our needs when we obey Him. These would be lessons that He has repeated throughout my life, each time stretching my faith a little further so I could grow.

Perhaps the Lord is cultivating your confidence in Him. If you are waiting for an important answer or His provision, keep listening and trusting no matter how long it takes. The Father will not fail you (Deut. 31:8).

5. Training Us to Hear His Voice

When I was growing up, I used to spend time after school with five of my buddies. We would go down to a big field close to our neighborhood and play for a few hours until dinnertime.

I remember how Mother would call me home to eat: "Charles! Charles! Time for supper!" That was my cue to head into the house and clean up. I wasn't confused when the other boys' moms would bid them to come in; I could easily identify my own mother's voice. Even when she didn't say my name, I knew it was her summoning me.

Likewise, God trains us to distinguish His voice from all others. You and I cannot obey Him unless we first learn to recognize His call.

Think about all of the messages we hear throughout the day. Some of them are godly—perhaps we read a devotional or listen to a Christian radio program that exalts the Lord and helps us to seek Him more faithfully. We also encounter negative, destructive ideas: those that cater to our flesh rather than to our spirit. If we do not discern which ones honor God and which don't, we may soon find ourselves heading down the wrong path.

The Father uses the silence to draw a sharp contrast between His counsel and the advice of others.

6. Teaching Us to Persevere in the Ultimate Conversation

The Lord is sometimes quiet because He is teaching us endurance in our relationships with Him. Jesus taught the disciples the parable of the persistent widow for just this purpose (Luke 18:1–8). The woman was in need of protection because of some conflict she was having. She repeatedly asked the judge to help her until he relented because of her tenacity. Likewise, God will "bring about justice for His elect who cry to Him day and night" (v. 7). He is faithful in answering our pleas.

Jesus taught them "that at all times they ought to pray and not to lose heart" (v. 1). Perseverance is crucial in our relationships with the Father because His timing is not like ours; nor are His ways comparable to our ways (Isa. 55:8–9). Sometimes He desires for us to wait because He is arranging our circumstances or protecting us from danger. He may be purifying our motives, teaching us to rely on Him, or preparing us to influence others.

The point is, He is working and has not abandoned us. We should heed the words of Hebrews 10:35–36: "Do not throw away your confidence, which has a great reward. For you have need of endurance, so that when you have done the will of God, you may receive what was promised."

HOW SHOULD WE RESPOND TO GOD'S SILENCE?

The truth of the matter is, every time of silence, trial, challenge, or need the Lord allows us to experience carries with it an opportunity for us to learn something from Him. Here are some important steps we can take to make sure we continue walking in the center of His will.

Ask the Lord Why He Is So Quiet

Is there something you should learn, a sin you must confess, or a step of obedience you can take? Use this time to examine your heart and recommit yourself to the Father. Ask Him:

- Lord, are You seeking to get my attention and refocus my mind on Your character?
- Are You preparing me to obey You—waiting until I am wholeheartedly committed to doing Your will?
- Is there iniquity in my life that You are revealing? Do I need to repent of any sinful behaviors?
- Are You growing my faith—teaching me lessons about how profoundly I can trust You?
- Are You training me to hear Your voice and discern Your truth in the midst of all the messages I'm bombarded with daily?
- Father, are You teaching me to persevere in this conversation with You?

Remember That God's Silence Doesn't Mean He's Inactive

Throughout history, the Father has used periods of silence to accomplish great things, such as setting the world stage for the coming of the Messiah. Therefore, meditate on such times and remember that He continues working on your behalf (Isa. 64:4).

Recall All the Ways the Lord Has Been Faithful to You

God has never let you down before, nor will He in the future. So think about all the times He's fought for you; provided for you; and shown you His power, wisdom, mercy, and love. Then, praise Him for all the good plans He has for your life.

Take This Opportunity to Be Completely Honest

Since God is all-knowing, your feelings won't surprise Him. Once you have openly expressed your heart to Him, you will be more receptive to His encouragement and direction.

Commit to Being Quiet Before the Lord Every Day

Whether you hear His voice or not, read the Bible, tell the Father you are available to listen, and wait silently for Him to speak. Make it a consistent habit that takes priority in your life. Eventually, you will have a breakthrough and will hear God more clearly and powerfully than you ever thought possible.

If the Father has been silent lately, you can be confident that He is calling you to a new level of intimacy. Therefore, do not be discouraged or afraid. Humble yourself before almighty God; get on your knees and acknowledge that He is Lord of your life. Recall all the ways He has been faithful to you. Wait quietly before Him, willing to hear and obey whatever

He says to you. Thank Him for being active on your behalf. Anticipate His awesome answer.

When you actively listen for His voice, the Lord is certain to respond. He will assuredly give you the profound sense of His presence, love, and power that you've been longing to experience.

Father, how grateful we are for You, even when You are silent. We know that You are accomplishing great things in our lives through times of quietness—drawing us closer in relationship with You, preparing us to obey, revealing our sins, training us to identify Your voice, teaching us to trust You, and building our endurance. Thank You, Lord, for the indescribable peace and joy that come from knowing You will never leave us nor forsake us.

Father, I pray specifically for this reader—that Your Holy Spirit will use this message to encourage this individual's heart. Your child longs to be in conversation with You, Lord, so I pray this dear soul will learn what You desire to teach through the silence.

May You be honored and glorified by all we say and do, Lord God. In Jesus' matchless and wonderful name, I pray. Amen.

9

∽

OVERCOMING OBSTACLES

Winning Your Battles on Your Knees

FIRST THESSALONIANS 5:17 INSTRUCTS US to "pray without ceasing," or to be in constant conversation with the Father. As we know, it is vital to seek the Lord's presence and direction in our lives. He understands what is best for us and has the wisdom and power to help us become everything He created us to be.

Interacting with God continuously is crucial when we experience trials and obstacles because our problems have a way of overwhelming and discouraging us. We lie awake at night, wondering, *Father, what am I going to do? Why have You allowed this in my life? I don't know how to go on.* We're not sure how to face the decisions and consequences that will come. The pain and emptiness of our difficulties can overpower us.

Perhaps you are experiencing some devastating circumstances today or see troubles on the horizon that will soon plague you. Maybe you lack a sense of direction or real purpose. You may wonder if you need to give up on your goals and dreams because you feel like you don't measure up and will never deserve the good things you desire.

At such times, you may be tempted to seek refuge in earthly comforts such as wealth, possessions, addictive substances, food, or sex. You may even wish to isolate yourself from the world and push everyone away. Don't. Each of these promises to comfort your hurting soul, but they will end up hurting you in the long run.

Instead, cling to the only One who can help you overcome your challenges: your heavenly Father. First Peter 5:7 admonishes, "Cast all your anxiety on Him, because He cares for you." You must entrust Him with your doubts and difficulties by continuing in the ultimate conversation with Him.

If we maintain focus on God during times of trial, adversity can become a bridge to a deeper relationship with Him.

If we maintain focus on God during times of trial, adversity can become a bridge to a deeper relationship with Him. The Lord may permit a problem far beyond your strength or abilities just so you will learn to rely upon Him moment by moment (2 Cor. 12:7–10).

As we've seen, every time of difficulty, challenge, or need the Father allows in our lives is an opportunity for us to learn something from Him. He wants you to know that you can rely upon Him, no matter what is going on.

TAKING TROUBLE TO THE
GREAT PROBLEM SOLVER

King Hezekiah of Judah offers an excellent example. Second Kings 18:5–6 tells us, "He trusted in the LORD, the God of Israel; so that after him there was none like him among all the kings of Judah. . . . He clung to the LORD; he did not depart from following Him." However, it was not always easy.

On the world stage during this era was the rise of a militarily powerful, cruel, and bloodthirsty people called the Assyrians under the leadership of Tiglath-Pilesar III (also known as Pul). Through his brutal tactics, he quickly conquered territories from Mesopotamia to the Mediterranean. He made Israel (2 Kings 15:19–20) and Judah (2 Kings 16:7–9) his vassals and demanded heavy tributes from them.

Hezekiah had been ruling the nation of Judah for only six years when Israel, his neighbor to the north and ally, rebelled against the Assyrians and fell to them in 722 B.C. The fallout was especially difficult for Hezekiah because the Israelites were the kinsmen of the Judahites. As was their practice, the Assyrians carried the Israelites into exile, separating them from their families and land, which weakened Judah both psychologically and in terms of national security.

Despite the immense setback, Hezekiah took his responsibility to obey God seriously, no matter how difficult submitting to His commands might be. One of the most problematic mandates was Deuteronomy 17:15: "You shall surely set a king over you whom the LORD your God chooses, one from among your countrymen you shall set as king over your-selves; you may not put a foreigner over yourselves who is not your countryman." In practical terms, Judah could no longer accept being under bondage to a foreign power. As long as the king of Assyria—which was Sennacherib by this time—ruled them, they would not be able to serve the Lord unhindered.

So Hezekiah humbled himself and trusted God. Second Kings 18:7 tells us, "He rebelled against the king of Assyria," most likely refusing to send any more tributes.

However, as sometimes happens, when we obey God, we also stir up the anger of His enemies.

---

c. 922 B.C.	The nation of Israel divides into the southern kingdom of Judah and the northern kingdom of Israel (1 Kings 12)
c. 745 B.C.	Assyria rises to power under the leadership of Tiglath-Pilesar III
c. 738 B.C.	Israel is forced to pay tribute to Assyria (2 Kings 15:19–20)
c. 733 B.C.	Judah begins paying tribute to Assyria (2 Kings 16:7–9)
c. 727 B.C.	Hezekiah begins co-regency of Judah with his father, Ahaz
c. 722 B.C.	Samaria, the capital of Israel, falls to the Assyrians (2 Kings 17, 18:9–11)
c. 714 B.C.	Hezekiah is the sole king of Judah
c. 701 B.C.	Sennacherib of Assyria invades Judah (Isa. 36–37)

Sennacherib did not take Hezekiah's rebellion lightly. In fact, Isaiah 36:1 reports, "In the fourteenth year of King Hezekiah, Sennacherib king of Assyria came up against all the fortified cities of Judah and seized them." He was able to conquer forty-six cities and subjugate them, stopping only when he got to Lachish, which was thirty miles southwest of Jerusalem. That cut off any aid from Egypt, should Hezekiah hope to seek reinforcements.

"With him is only an arm of flesh, but with us is the LORD our God to help us and to fight our battles." (2 Chron. 32:8)

Hezekiah remained firm. He told the people, "Be strong and courageous, do not fear or be dismayed because of the king of Assyria nor because of all the horde that is with him; for the one with us is greater than the one with him. With him is only an arm of flesh, but with us is the LORD our God to help us and to fight our battles" (2 Chron. 32:7–8). His statement heartened the people, but unfortunately, not for long.

Seeing their dependence on the Lord, Sennacherib sent three of his commanders—Tartan, Rabsaris, and Rabshakeh—and an army of approximately 185,000 soldiers to Jerusalem. Their goal was to force the Judahites to surrender by waging psychological warfare. If they could not turn Hezekiah away from God, perhaps they could scare the people of Judah into rebelling against him.

Rabshakeh stood and cried with a loud voice in Judean, saying, "Hear the word of the great king, the king of

Assyria. Thus says the king, 'Do not let Hezekiah deceive you, for he will not be able to deliver you from my hand; nor let Hezekiah make you trust in the LORD, saying, "The LORD will surely deliver us, and this city will not be given into the hand of the king of Assyria."

'Do not listen to Hezekiah, for thus says the king of Assyria, "*Make your peace with me and come out to me, and eat each of his vine and each of his fig tree and drink each of the waters of his own cistern, until I come and take you away to a land like your own land, a land of grain and new wine, a land of bread and vineyards, a land of olive trees and honey, that you may live and not die.*"

'But do not listen to Hezekiah when he misleads you, saying, "The LORD will deliver us." Has any one of the gods of the nations delivered his land from the hand of the king of Assyria? Where are the gods of Hamath and Arpad? Where are the gods of Sepharvaim, Hena and Ivvah? Have they delivered Samaria from my hand? *Who among all the gods of the lands have delivered their land from my hand, that the LORD* should deliver Jerusalem from my hand?' " (2 Kings 18:28–35, emphasis added)

How often does this happen to us? We take a stand for God, and suddenly, our faith is attacked. We state our absolute trust in the Father, and the next thing we know, doubts flood our mind.

As for Hezekiah and the people of Jerusalem, they could have taken those threats to heart. After all, Israel had not been able to stand against Assyria, and neither had those forty-six cities in Judah that had already fallen. Why should they expect the fate of Jerusalem to be any different?

Wasn't the Assyrian army stronger than their forces? How could they possibly stand against an undefeated world power? Would God really help them? What if He was angry with them? Perhaps He was chastising Judah for some reason, as He had punished Israel (2 Kings 17:7–18). Could they count on Him to deliver them? Maybe they should accept Sennacherib's offer—surrender and live prosperously under Assyrian rule.

Thankfully, instead of contemplating his doubts, Hezekiah went to the place we should all go when troubles assail us: to the Great Problem Solver. He sought God's guidance, praying,

> O LORD, the God of Israel, who are enthroned above the cherubim, You are the God, You alone, of all the kingdoms of the earth. You have made heaven and earth. Incline Your ear, O LORD, and hear; open Your eyes, O LORD, and see; and *listen to the words of Sennacherib, which he has sent to reproach the living God.* Truly, O LORD, the kings of Assyria have devastated the nations and their lands and have cast their gods into the fire, *for they were not gods but the work of men's* hands, wood and stone. So they have destroyed them. Now, O LORD our God, I pray, *deliver us from his hand that all the kingdoms of the earth may know that You alone, O LORD,* are God. (2 Kings 19:15–19, emphasis added)

Hezekiah fought this battle on his knees, seeking the Father's provision to deliver Jerusalem. He recognized that the Assyrians could conquer only other nations whose deities "were not gods but the work of men's hands" (v. 18). But the armies of Sennacherib could not possibly stand against the living God! Here was an opportunity to show the whole world who the Lord of all creation truly was.

"Deliver us from his hand that all the kingdoms of the earth may know that You alone, O LORD, are God."

(2 Kings 19:19)

And the Father honored his prayer. Through the prophet Isaiah, God told Hezekiah that Sennacherib would return to his land and be killed with the sword (2 Kings 19:6–7; Isa. 37:6–7). Also, the army would not even be able to shoot an arrow at Jerusalem (2 Kings 19:32–33). The Lord would defend them.

As always, the Father was true to His word. When the people of Jerusalem awoke the next day, the angel of the Lord had struck dead the 185,000 soldiers of the Assyrian army—they never had the chance to place arrows on their bowstrings. Later, as God said, Sennacherib was assassinated by two of his sons while he was worshipping his deity (2 Kings 19:35–37; Isa. 37:36–38).

There is evidence that Psalm 46 was written after this great victory, a fitting tribute to how the Lord delivered Jerusalem:

God is our refuge and strength,
A very present help in trouble.

Therefore we will not fear, though the earth should
    change
And though the mountains slip into the heart of the
    sea . . .
Make glad the city of God,
The holy dwelling places of the Most High.
God is in the midst of her, she will not be moved;
God will help her when morning dawns. . . .
"Cease striving and know that I am God;
I will be exalted among the nations, I will be exalted
    in the earth."
The LORD of hosts is with us;
The God of Jacob is our stronghold. (vv. 1 2, 4–5,
    10–11)

WHAT DOES THIS MEAN TO YOU?

You and I most likely will not face Assyrian armies anytime soon, but there are principles in Hezekiah's example that we can remember whenever we face troubles that are far greater than we can handle. No matter what obstacles or challenges we encounter, we don't have to endure them alone. Rather, like Hezekiah, we should turn to the Great Problem Solver and trust Him to help us.

1. *God Is Interested in Your Problems*

The first thing we need to realize is that as believers and children of the living God, the Father will help us overcome anything that is defeating, discouraging, or depressing us. He wants us to talk to Him about our concerns. And He desires us to seek His counsel and guidance.

We may understand this as a theological point. But I say it first and foremost because at times our difficulties may make us feel insignificant, inadequate, and unworthy. We may feel we are below the Father's notice. After all, He has the entire world to care for; why should He spend time on the issues that distress individuals? When the world is facing ongoing conflict in the Middle East, famine, natural disasters, and entire nations engaged in civil war, why should He waste His efforts addressing the small burdens with which we wrestle?

Let me remind you: The ultimate conversation is about your *intimate* walk with the Lord. Jesus said, "The very hairs of your head are all numbered" (Matt. 10:29). That means the Father cares about each detail of your daily interaction with Him, and He wants you to be in deep fellowship with Him regarding every area of your life.

If it concerns you, it matters to Him.

Never say, "God doesn't care about *that*." He does. If it concerns you, it matters to Him. Therefore, as Psalm 62:8 instructs, "Trust in Him at all times, O people; pour out your heart before Him; God is a refuge for us."

2. The Lord Is Greater Than Your Difficulties

We have talked about the fact that the Father is omnipotent, omniscient, and omnipresent, and loves us unconditionally. Though we may accept these facts intellectually, the important thing is to apply them to our circumstances in a practical way. Whenever we face times of trial, we must honestly ask ourselves: *Do I trust that God is able to handle any problem I experience?*

The Father never wrings His hands when you go to Him with a challenging situation. He is capable of leading you to victory, regardless of what you face.

He asks the rhetorical question, "I am the LORD, the God of all flesh; is anything too difficult for Me?" (Jer. 32:27). Absolutely not. He was able to create all of humankind from dust—with our immensely intricate biological systems, distinctive physical attributes, unique personality traits, and different spiritual gifts (Gen. 2:7). The God who can do that can take care of any issue that concerns us.

> *Though our struggles may appear insurmountable or unending to us, to the Lord they are simply an opportunity to draw us closer.*

Though our struggles may appear insurmountable or unending to us, to the Lord they are simply an opportunity to draw us closer to Him and to teach us to rely upon Him more. The question is: Can we stop trying to manage our circumstances? Can we let go of control, allowing Him to do as He intends?

The question of control was a difficult one for Hezekiah. The Assyrians were offering peace, protection, and prosperity (2 Kings 18:23, 31–32). But if he refused them, they promised to attack, killing or deporting all the inhabitants of Jerusalem. Would Hezekiah heed the threats of the very real army before

You don't have to handle your difficulties with your own imperfect strength. Let go and allow God to deliver you.

him or the promises of the unseen God of his forefathers? Humanly speaking, the easy way out would have been to comply with the Assyrians' demands.

Thankfully, Hezekiah didn't take the easy route—he chose the *right* one. He believed the Lord and witnessed the mighty liberation of Jerusalem.

Decisions such as these either grow or undermine our faith. Either we will trust the Father, as Hezekiah did, and see the awesome, supernatural provision of the living Lord; or we won't, and we will be forced to live with the devastating consequences of our choices. Friend, you don't have to handle your difficulties with your own imperfect strength. Let go and allow God to deliver you.

3. Seek the Father Before You Go to Others

Let me ask you: In times of crisis, do you initially turn to the Lord? Or do you immediately contact a friend? Do you go to your knees in prayer or to your phone to call someone?

One of the ways we unintentionally shut the Lord out of

our problems is to talk about our circumstances with loved ones, allowing them to shape our view of the situation. Suddenly, our struggles appear far larger and more out of hand than they are. We consider all the paths we could take and the potential outcomes. Eventually, the scenarios become jumbled in our minds—we forget what is reality and what is merely supposition. The more we discuss our dilemma with others, the more confused we become.

Our first step should be to turn to the Father. As 1 Corinthians 14:33 reminds us, "God is not a God of confusion but of peace." The Lord wants to lead us to the best course of action and will do so if we seek Him.

That is not to say we should never consult with others. No Christian has ever been called to "go it alone" in his or her walk of faith. Scripture tells us, "In abundance of counselors there is victory" (Prov. 11:14). We should talk to godly people whom we trust and respect. Of course, we must also be cautious about whom we entrust with our concerns. We should make sure that our confidants are not only focused on God but will be discreet about what we share with them.

The Lord may show us with whom to speak. Someone else may be going through the same trial, and this is an opportunity for you to encourage and support each other. You can help carry each other's burdens, and seeing God answer your prayers can increase your faith.

One of the greatest treasures in life is a Christ-centered, caring friend who will walk with you through the trying times and approach the throne of grace on your behalf. However, I challenge you to develop the habit of going to the Father *first* with your problems. As His child, you have the incredible privilege of seeking Him to alleviate your burdens (Ps. 55:22). Let Him put your difficulties in perspective and direct you. Then you can discuss what He shows you with a friend who will support you with prayer and godly advice.

4. The Lord Will Provide the Best Solution for Your Difficulty

When you can come to the place where you know God is interested in your problem, that He is greater than anything you could ever face, and that He knows exactly what to do, your troubles will get smaller and less intimidating. Why? Because you're focused on the Lord: your all-powerful, all-knowing, ever-present, and completely loving Father.

He not only has the best plan to overcome your struggles; He is also using your struggles in the wisest way possible in order to build you up. As Romans 8:28 reminds us: "We know that God causes all things to work together for good to those who love God, to those who are called according to His purpose." He understands your emotional and spiritual makeup—exactly what you need to grow closer to Him, mature in your faith, and be "conformed to the image of His Son" (Rom. 8:29).

Even if His solution is slow in coming, or His answer requires you to take a step of faith, you can be certain that it will result in deeper peace, joy, and contentment than you've ever known. You are also assured that your trust in the Father's plans and purposes will result in eternal blessings. When you stand before Him on judgment day, you will be rewarded for your obedience (Luke 6:21–23).

When you pray, do you tend to focus on your problem— its details, severity, and possible conse- quences? Or do you believe the Father is able to help you overcome any impasse? Are you willing to address this obstacle in conversation with the Lord? I can assure you that if you will choose to focus on His resources, greatness, and love, your tribula- tions will seem smaller and less frightening.

Focus on the Father's awesome power, and trust Him to resolve your situation in His timing. In His hands, problems aren't roadblocks—they are awesome opportu- nities for you to develop a more intimate and dynamic relationship with Him.

> *In His hands, problems aren't roadblocks—they are awesome opportunities for you to develop a more intimate and dynamic relationship with Him.*

HOW TO FIGHT YOUR BATTLES

Perhaps you're wondering what you should do when it is not a mere setback you're facing but an all-out war; when there are no easy solutions, no ways to avoid the tsunami of troubles headed your way. The trial ahead is life-altering and distressing and could affect your entire future and that of those you love.

You may have heard me say that we must fight such battles on our knees. What exactly does that mean? What does that conversation with God look like?

Just as Hezekiah did, we must put away our swords, strategies, and earthly resources—as well as our rights to engage the conflicts on our terms—and allow the Lord to be our commander in chief.

Why? In such cases: "Our struggle is not against flesh and blood, but against the rulers, against the powers, against the world forces of this darkness, against the spiritual forces of wickedness in the heavenly places" (Eph. 6:12). We are engaged not in a solely human dispute but in an effort with profound eternal ramifications that must be addressed spiritually (2 Cor. 10:4–5).

It may seem counterintuitive and even somewhat irresponsible to let go and pray when you encounter a battle so deep and overwhelming that it feels as if everything in your life is against you. But when you face a seemingly no-win situation, your best course of action is *always* to turn to the Father.

I say this as a matter of experience. I've endured many challenges throughout my life, and they've all shown me that fighting battles on our knees is one of the most important and powerful lessons we can ever learn as believers.

One of my greatest struggles began a year and a half after I was called to First Baptist Atlanta as the associate pastor. The senior pastor had resigned, and several members of the pulpit committee suggested that I fill his role. As I prayed about it, God showed me it was His will for me to be senior pastor of the church. I continued to serve—preaching every Sunday morning and evening—as the committee deliberated. First Baptist began to change and grow spiritually. It was obvious that the Lord was at work.

That was when the conflict arose. Seven affluent and influential members of the congregation didn't like either the fact that I sought the Father's direction in every decision or the way I taught from God's Word. They began to spread false, vicious accusations about me. Sadly, many people believed their fabrications and joined in the effort to get rid of me.

The tension continued to escalate in the months that followed. This group even sent three attorneys to threaten me, saying, "If you don't resign quietly and walk away from here, we'll make sure you never pastor another church."

I remember how difficult and disheartening it was to walk out on Sunday morning and preach, knowing that so many church members bitterly despised everything I said and represented. I recall going to the prayer room often, even telling God that I didn't want to be their pastor. During that time, the Father taught me that I could rely upon Him, no matter who rejected me.

God said, "If you want to win this battle, you must fight it on your knees alone with Me. Do not argue or stand up for yourself. Remain faithful to Me. I will protect you."

God said, "If you want to win this battle, you must fight it on your knees alone with Me." He made it very clear:

"Do not argue or stand up for yourself. Remain faithful to Me. I will protect you."

He also gave me Isaiah 54:17 as a promise: "No weapon that is formed against you will prosper; and every tongue that accuses you in judgment you will condemn. This is the heritage of the servants of the LORD, and their vindication is from Me."

More than forty years later, I can say with great joy that the Father has been absolutely faithful in fulfilling everything He taught and promised me. He fought for me, safeguarded me, and triumphed in that impossible situation.

DEPENDING ON YOUR DEFENDER

If there is a challenge you're facing and people or circumstances are aligned against you, how can you fight the battle on your knees? How can you overcome the difficulty while remaining faithful to the Father?

1. Set Aside Time Alone with the Father

First, do not allow anything to interrupt your time with the Lord. If anything, your moments apart with Him should increase, not decrease.

It is easy to be distracted when conflicts arise. You can become so busy fretting about your troubles and running after solutions that you fail to turn to the One who can best help you (Ps. 37:5–9). You may be tempted to blame the Lord for allowing the trial in your life. Remember, He knows your future and all the people who will be affected eternally because of your obedience to Him.

There may be some aspect of training you need that can come only through this kind of challenge. Perhaps He is increasing your understanding of certain types of suffering so you will be a better minister of the gospel (2 Cor. 1:3–7). It could be that there are areas of your life that are not yet submitted to His will, and He is using a hardship to help you come to a point of total surrender. Whatever the case, you can be certain that He is not letting you down but edifying you.

> *Remember, He knows your future and all the people who will be affected eternally because of your obedience to Him.*

Schedule time to focus solely on the Father. Let nothing come before your communion with Him because it is crucial to your success.

2. Listen Quietly to the Lord and Expect Him to Speak to You

During my time of difficulty, I depended heavily on God to direct my steps. I knew that only He could see the entire road ahead and know where all the traps were planted.

As David wrote, "Those who seek my life lay snares for me; and those who seek to injure me have threatened destruction, and they devise treachery all day long. But I, like a deaf man, do not hear; and I am like a mute man who does not open his mouth. . . . For I hope in You, O LORD; You will answer, O Lord my God" (Ps. 38:12–13, 15).

Likewise, God wants to guide you in the way you should go so He can safeguard you. Do not defend yourself or rally people to your side. Simply trust the Lord. He has a better perspective on what is happening than you do, and He can keep you safe. All you must do is pay attention to Him and obey His direction, because "the Lord will go before you, and the God of Israel will be your rear guard" (Isa. 52:12). He will protect you on every side.

3. If the Lord Reveals Any Sinfulness in Your Life, Repent of It Immediately

Whenever there is conflict or confusion in our lives, we should always examine ourselves for how we've contributed to the turmoil. Are we facing the consequences of our sinful behavior? Is there anyone we should ask to forgive us? Is there any restitution we should make? We must ensure that our hearts are clean and pure before God if we hope to triumph in the situation.

> *We must ensure that our hearts are clean and pure before God if we hope to triumph in the situation.*

Remember, the Father's primary goal is to have an intimate relationship with you. When sin is present, it is evidence that you are preventing Him from having full access to your life. The psalmist wrote, "If I had cherished sin in my heart, the Lord would not have listened; but God has surely listened and has heard my prayer" (Ps. 66:18–19 NIV). The Father will not compete to be Master of your life. He wants you to choose Him above your transgressions.

Agree with God about your iniquity, and allow Him to teach you. He will show you how to change the way you operate for maximum intimacy with Him, effectiveness in your life, and influence with others.

4. Remember, There Can Be Only One General in This Battle—the Lord

As I wrote earlier in this chapter, when we fight our battles on our knees, we no longer depend on our own weapons, strategies, abilities, or resources. We give up the right to engage the conflict on our terms or to find our own solutions. Instead, we allow the Father to be our commander in chief.

David wrote, "I know that the LORD saves His anointed; He will answer him from His holy heaven with the saving strength of His right hand. Some boast in chariots and some in horses, but we will boast in the name of the LORD, our God. They have bowed down and fallen, but we have risen and stood upright" (Ps. 20:6–8).

God willingly employs His supernatural power in defending you, training you, and bringing out your full potential. However, you must be willing to acknowledge that He is in control and knows the path ahead better than you do. In order to achieve the victory God has envisioned, you must surrender yourself to Him fully.

> *In order to achieve the victory God has envisioned, you must surrender yourself to Him fully.*

This may mean stepping out in faith when it is extremely uncomfortable or even petrifying to do so (Josh. 6). You may need to temporarily abandon some of your goals in order to seek the objectives that the Lord has for you (1 Sam. 24). No matter how much discomfort His commands cause you, obey Him anyway. Agree to trust the Father's direction, knowing wholeheartedly that "WHOEVER BELIEVES IN HIM WILL NOT BE DISAPPOINTED" (Rom. 10:11). He is a faithful, skilled general who has never lost a battle and will not let you down.

5. Know That People Are Never Your Enemy—Sin Is

At times your trials will be the result of other people's actions, as mine were at First Baptist. During those difficult seasons, remember that each person is loved by God and needs Jesus to be his or her Savior. If those opposing you are believers, they are also your brothers and sisters in Christ.

The Lord is clear: "If someone says, 'I love God,' and hates his brother, he is a liar; for the one who does not love his brother whom he has seen, cannot love God whom he has not seen" (1 John 4:20). For this reason, we must make every effort to make sure no anger, bitterness, or unforgiveness takes root in our hearts. Rather, we are called to love others as Christ loved us: with compassion, mercy, grace, and forgiveness (Luke 23:34; Eph. 4:32). In caring for them, we show our devotion to the Father (Matt. 25:34–40; John 13:34–35).

People are not our enemies; sin is. And if we fight our battles on our knees, God will not only help us be victorious, He will also redeem those who oppose us. Therefore, we should never act in a manner that would disgrace the name of Jesus or hinder others from following Him in obedience. The goal is always to lead whomever we come in contact with back to faith and trust in Christ.

6. Understand That the Dark Moments of Your Life Last Only as Long as Necessary

Though it is true that we will continue to fight some battles throughout our lives, we make a terrible mistake when we look at our circumstances and think, *Things will never change.* There is nothing so discouraging as being convinced a difficult situation cannot or will not improve.

Such a faulty assumption usually comes from a wrong view about God's character or His ability to redeem us. Either we perceive Him as a cruel taskmaster who delights in our sorrows, or we see ourselves as so broken that we deserve no better. I

> *We make a terrible mistake when we look at our circumstances and think,* Things will never change.

assure you, disheartenment and defeat are never God's will for His people.

In Lamentations 3:32–33, we are taught, "If He causes grief, then He will have compassion according to His abundant loving-kindness. For He does not afflict willingly or grieve the sons of men."

The Father does not want to cause us heartache. He does so only to release us from the bondage of sin or to prevent us from experiencing more terrible suffering later on. Like a surgery to extract a cancerous tumor, the procedure may be painful, but it is worth the price to remove the object that is killing us.

God also allows adversity for the purpose of teaching us to serve Him. So when we endure trials that equip us for more effective service to Him, we must think of ourselves as spiritual athletes in training (1 Cor. 9:23–25; 2 Tim. 2:5). He exercises our faith, perseverance, and hope—spiritual muscles that enable us to "run with endurance the race that is set before us" (Heb. 12:1).

This training does not go on forever. Adversity lasts only as long as is necessary for the Father to accomplish His purpose in your life. In other words, God limits the heartache and pain you experience. He knows what you can handle and what you need. Do not be discouraged. Rather, take heart that what He is producing in you is both extremely valuable and eternal (2 Cor. 4:16–18).

7. See Everything That Happens to You as Coming from God

One of the most important lessons the Father has taught me is to see all adversity as coming from Him for my good. Through our trials, He draws us closer to Him, conforms us to the character of Christ, prepares us for ministry, reveals our sin, and strengthens our faith. Understanding this truth protects us from bitterness, resentment, and hostility toward those who wrong us (Gen. 50:20). It also prevents us from becoming disheartened when trials assail us.

See all adversity as coming from the Father for your good.

Earlier in this chapter, we examined the truth of Romans 8:28, which says, "We know that God causes all things to work together for good to those who love God, to those who are called according to His purpose." You and I may experience earthly losses during a battle, but if the struggle brings us to the point of total surrender to the Lord, we can consider it a spiritual victory.

Likewise, other promises throughout Scripture demonstrate the purifying and edifying effects of adversity:

- "He knows the way I take; when He has tried me, I shall come forth as gold." (Job 23:10)
- "It is good for me that I was afflicted, that I may learn Your statutes." (Ps. 119:71)

- "Although the Lord has given you bread of privation and water of oppression, *He,* your Teacher will no longer hide Himself, but your eyes will behold your Teacher. Your ears will hear a word behind you, 'This is the way, walk in it,' whenever you turn to the right or to the left." (Isa. 30:20–21)

- "Though the fig tree should not blossom and there be no fruit on the vines, though the yield of the olive should fail and the fields produce no food, though the flock should be cut off from the fold and there be no cattle in the stalls, yet I will exult in the LORD, I will rejoice in the God of my salvation. The Lord GOD is my strength, and He has made my feet like hinds' feet, and makes me walk on my high places." (Hab. 3:17–19)

- "I will bring the third part through the fire, refine them as silver is refined, and test them as gold is tested. They will call on My name, and I will answer them; I will say, 'They are My people,' and they will say, 'The LORD is my God.' " (Zech. 13:9)

- "We exult in hope of the glory of God. And not only this, but we also exult in our tribulations, knowing that tribulation brings about perseverance; and perseverance, proven character; and proven character, hope; and hope does not disappoint, because the love of God has been poured out within our hearts through the Holy Spirit who was given to us." (Rom. 5:2–5)

- "Consider it all joy, my brethren, when you encounter various trials, knowing that the testing of your faith produces endurance. And let endurance have its perfect result, so that you may be perfect and complete, lacking in nothing." (James 1:2–4)

- "In this you greatly rejoice, even though now for a little while, if necessary, you have been distressed by various trials, so that the proof of your faith, being more precious than gold which is perishable, even though tested by fire, may be found to result in praise and glory and honor at the revelation of Jesus Christ." (1 Pet. 1:6–7)

If the Father allows a trial or challenge in your life, you can be certain it is ultimately for your good and His glory. Knowing that He has permitted the troubles in your life for your benefit makes it easier to forgive those who hurt you and to endure your difficulties as long as you must bear them.

THE PURPOSE OF FASTING IN THE ULTIMATE CONVERSATION

It is usually at this point that someone will ask me about the place of fasting in our interactions with the Father. Often the inquiry into this spiritual discipline is fueled by a desire to relieve the stress of a particular trial; at times a person sincerely wants to know God's will in his or her situation. The person will ask: "Should a person fast when experiencing problems like this one? Does it help at all?"

Absolutely. Fasting can be one of the most powerful, most profoundly intimate experiences of the Christian life.

> *Fasting can be one of the most powerful, most profoundly intimate experiences of the Christian life.*

Fasting means abstaining from something for the purpose of devoting that time to seeking the Lord—His direction and will for our lives. Usually, it means giving up food, sleep, or a favorite pastime, such as watching television, so we can be undisturbed in hearing the Father. The idea is that if we remove the things that have our attention, we can focus on God more effectively.

Sadly, there is a lot of confusion about this excellent spiritual practice. Instead of seeing it as an opportunity to interact with the Father more deeply, some believe it is a religious ritual meant to impress Him with their intensity of devotion to Him. Others hope their self-denial will either speed up the Lord's answer or influence Him to respond to a request in a certain way. Some even use fasting as a diet plan.

None of these reflects the biblical purpose of fasting. Jesus said:

"Whenever you fast, do not put on a gloomy face as the hypocrites *do,* for they neglect their appearance so that they will be noticed by men when they are fasting. Truly I say to you, they have their reward in full. But you, when you fast, anoint your head and wash your face so that your fasting will not be noticed by men, but by your Father who is in secret; and your Father who sees *what is done* in secret will reward you." (Matt. 6:16–18)

In other words, you and I should never fast with the intention of impressing anyone or persuading the Father to do things our way. That's not its purpose. Rather, we fast to prepare our hearts to accomplish God's will, to focus on the Lord's presence so we can hear His voice and understand how He wants us to proceed. This is our reward.

It will be fruitless to fast unless our goal is intimacy with the Father. As we submit ourselves to Him, He replaces our agenda with His own. He deals with us, surfacing our wounds, sins, and destructive habits so we can be free of them. Why? Because you and I are most effective when we are pure of heart. As we connect with Him and embrace all of what He shows us, He demonstrates His unconditional love in ways we've never experienced before.

Will fasting help you during times of difficulty? Does this spiritual discipline make a difference? Yes. Fasting focuses your attention on the Father as you fight your battles on your knees. And this, my friend, is a recipe for victory, regardless of what challenges you encounter.

WIN THIS BATTLE WITH YOUR EYES ON GOD

One more thing about that contentious season at First Baptist that I hope will bless you: During that time, I frequently felt lonely and helpless. Loneliness is often a by-product of our struggles—they isolate us from others because we feel no one understands what we're experiencing. The pain goes so deep and the insecurities can be so overwhelming that we doubt anyone has ever felt as insignificant or low as we do. Yet we're not alone. We never really are.

Focus your attention on the Father as you fight your battles on your knees. That's a recipe for victory regardless of what challenges you encounter.

One day during that very dark season, the Father encouraged me greatly through a dear lady in her eighties named Mrs. Sauls. She showed me a beautiful portrait of Daniel in the lion's den, a copy of a work that was painted by Briton Rivière in the 1890s.

Mrs. Sauls quietly said, "Son, look at that picture. I want you to tell me what you see." I described the scene, which showed the lions gathered behind Daniel, their mouths closed and bones all over the floor. Daniel appeared unconcerned.

He held his hands behind his back, and he looked up at the light that streamed in through the barred window of his cell.

She asked, "Is there anything else?"

I replied, "No ma'am." I will never forget what she said next—it was one of the wisest sermons I'd ever heard.

Mrs. Sauls put her arm around my waist and said, "Son, Daniel doesn't have his eyes on the lions. He has them on God." I tell you, it was as if the Father were hugging me, filling me with strength and comfort.

You see, Daniel had been wrongly accused, just as I had been (Dan. 6). His enemies had tricked King Darius into punishing him for worshipping God. The sentence was death by lions. Despite his terrible circumstances, he kept his eyes fixed upon the Lord and was miraculously saved.

I felt as if God was promising me that He would triumph in my battle just as He had done for Daniel. That message heartened me that day long ago. I'm recalling it today for the purpose of encouraging you.

Keep your eyes on the Father, and He will lead you to victory.

If you want to win the battles you experience, you must fight them on your knees alone with God. Do not argue or stand up for yourself. Remain faithful to Him, and He will protect you. Keep your eyes on the Father, rather than on whatever situation may arise, and He will lead you to victory.

Let me ask you: Are you facing a devastating trial today? Do you lie awake at night, wondering, *Father, what am I going to do? I don't know how to go on.* Are the pain and emptiness caused by your problems overpowering you?

If so, I challenge you to read the story of Daniel 6, when the man of God faced the lions' den by keeping his eyes on the Lord. Then cling to your heavenly Father. Fight this battle on your knees—not with your weapons, strategies, or resources but with faith in God. Entrust Him with your doubts and difficulties by continuing in the ultimate conversation with Him. Invite the Lord to be your Redeemer, Defender, General, Lion Tamer, and Protector. It's not only the best way to win, it's the most wonderful, eternal path to triumph every single time.

Father, how grateful we are for Your indescribable love. Truly, there is no Defender, Warrior, or King like You, in heaven or on earth. Regardless of the obstacles in our way, You overcome them easily. No matter the conflicts and trials we face, You are always triumphant.

Father, I pray especially for this dear reader today. May the doubts and difficulties that assail drive this individual into deeper, more consistent conversation with You. May this person learn the wonderful blessing of being able to fight every battle on his or her knees in prayer and with complete dependence on You.

Lord, thank You for always being available to us. Help us to wait on Your perfect timing, trust You every step of the way, and be willing to obey all You ask.

In Jesus' wonderful, holy, and powerful name, I pray. Amen.

10

~~

TALKING TO GOD ON
BEHALF OF OTHERS

How to Know You Are Praying God's Will

RECENTLY, I SPOKE TO A viewer who had wrestled with a prayer burden for over thirty-five years. One of her long-time friends had a daughter who was lost and in desperate need of Jesus as her Savior. You can probably understand how devastating it was for this mother and her friend as the years and decades went by. This young lady made mistake after mistake, trying to fill her deep need for God with things that simply could not satisfy. The more others would try to tell her about the life-changing love of Jesus, the further she would run from them and from the Father.

They finally realized that they would have to fight this battle on their knees. They remained faithful to intercede for this girl and trusted the Lord to hear and answer their prayers. But they had been praying for a very long time. As you can imagine, their hopes grew slim that this woman would be saved.

One day the friend's daughter came to see this viewer. It was a surprise, but she invited the young lady in and asked her to sit down. There was something different in the girl's face. There was some sadness, but there was a new softness and peace in her countenance.

Tears began flowing almost at once as the young woman admitted, "I have made a terrible mistake in my life. I rejected God because I thought He had something to do with the abuse I experienced in my childhood. I would cry out to Him, asking, 'Why did You let it happen? Why didn't You protect me?' Then I realized I only survived that trauma because He loved me and carried me through it. I came here today because I know you have been trying to tell me about His love for years and that you've been faithful to pray for me. And I wanted you to know that I've surrendered my life to the Lord. Jesus is my Savior."

As that faithful prayer warrior told me her story, she smiled from ear to ear. She said, "I cannot tell you the joy that filled my heart. I had prayed in earnest and with so many tears for that child. I had started to wonder if the Lord would allow me to live long enough to see her get right with Him. When the day came that she told me she had received Christ as her Savior, I experienced the greatest sense of victory and release I have ever felt. What a wise and wonderful God we serve!" Indeed He is.

Have you ever sensed that deep a prayer burden for another person? Perhaps there is someone in your life in a similar situation—a soul in desperate need of Christ as Savior. The years have gone by, and you long to see him or her embrace the gospel, but for whatever reason that person runs away from any mention of God.

Or maybe there are people you know who are in deep pain and need the Father's loving comfort and instruction. They want to break free from the bondage they're in but either don't realize how to or are afraid to step out in faith. How do you intercede for them without getting in the way of what the Lord is accomplishing in them?

There may even be a young man or woman in your circle of influence who is obviously called into the ministry, set apart to serve the Father. Ahead of that person is life at its best, building the kingdom of God. But you understand the future will hold challenges—trials that will stretch his or her confidence in the Lord and break any self-will. How can you pray for this person? How do you accept the necessity of the Father's training and discipline, no matter how difficult it is to watch?

How do you intercede for people without getting in the way of what the Lord is accomplishing in them?

PRAYING FOR OTHERS

It is possible that you're confused as to *why* God would call you to pray for another person. James 5:16 instructs, "Pray for one another so that you may be healed. The effective prayer of a righteous man can accomplish much."

If this ultimate conversation is about your intimate walk with the Father, then why should you talk about others while interacting with Him? Why would He give you a burden for another individual or group of people?

There are several reasons:

1. Looking Beyond Ourselves

First, the Father's unconditional love is focused outward, always seeking our good. So as we grow in His character, we are to be the same—compassionately caring for others in His name. As Jesus said, "By this all men will know that you are My disciples, if you have love for one another" (John 13:35).

> *The Lord asks us to intercede for others, not just for their benefit but so we can grow in His likeness.*

Remember, no Christian has ever been called to "go it alone" in his or her walk of faith. We need one another to grow in our relationships with God. The Lord asks us to intercede for others in order to help us move beyond our own concerns to the spiritual, physical, emotional, and relational needs of others. This is not just for their benefit but so we can grow in His likeness as well.

2. Caring for the Worldwide Body of Christ

Second, the Lord wants us to be aware of believers around the world who are actively preaching the gospel amid serious persecution. This was the case with the Thessalonians (Acts 17:1–9), who were ostracized and mistreated by many in their community.

In his second letter to them, Paul wrote:

> We ought always to give thanks to God for you, brethren, as is only fitting, because your faith is greatly enlarged, and the love of each one of you toward one another grows ever greater; therefore, *we ourselves speak proudly of you among the churches of God for your perseverance and faith in the midst of all your persecutions and afflictions which you endure.* . . . To this end also we pray for you always, *that our God will count you worthy of your calling, and fulfill every desire for goodness and the work of faith with power, so that the name of our Lord Jesus will be glorified in you, and you in Him,* according to the grace of our God and the Lord Jesus Christ. (2 Thess. 1:3–4, 11–12, emphasis added)

Likewise, we should intercede for Christians around the world who are suffering because of their faith. The Lord uses our conversation with Him to knit us together as a spiritual family, to unite our hearts in the purpose of proclaiming the Good News of salvation through Jesus Christ, and to lead the lost to know God personally.

Understanding their bold confidence in the Lord in the midst of oppression gives us the courage to persevere in our own times of adversity. As we intercede for them, the Lord makes us aware of their needs and works through us to provide for them (2 Cor. 8; James 2:15–16).

3. Receiving a Portion of the Blessing

Third, God wants us to pray for one another because He wants us to share in the joy that comes when He answers our requests, whether He meets someone's needs or leads that person to victory in a difficult situation. Our triumphs are sweeter and sorrows more bearable when we have someone with which to share them.

> *Our triumphs are sweeter and sorrows more bearable when we have someone with which to share them.*

For this reason, Romans 12:15 instructs, "Rejoice with those who rejoice, and weep with those who weep." We receive comfort from knowing we are not alone in our trials—that we have loved ones who will help us bear our burdens, just as we will for them (Gal. 6:2). And when we see God answering our prayers on behalf of others, our faith grows; we know He will fulfill His promises to us as well.

4. Preventing and Cleansing Us from Sin

Fourth, Jesus teaches us: "Love your enemies and pray for those who persecute you, so that you may be sons of your Father who is in heaven; for He causes His sun to rise on the evil and the good, and sends rain on the righteous and the unrighteous" (Matt. 5:44–45).

As we have discussed, unforgiveness is extremely destructive. I know people who have spent years in bondage to their bitterness and resentment.

When we intercede for those who oppose us, we invite God's compassion for them into our hearts. Instead of plotting how we will avenge ourselves of what they've done, we ask the Father to help them align with His will. Thus, we protect our hearts from sin, and we also pray in His will.

> *When we intercede for those who oppose us, we invite God's compassion for them into our hearts.*

5. Drawing Closer to God

The final reason the Lord may burden us with concern for another person is simply to draw us closer to Him. Paul exhibited this profound care for Timothy, his son in the faith. He wrote:

To Timothy, my beloved son: Grace, mercy and peace from God the Father and Christ Jesus our Lord. I thank

God, whom I serve with a clear conscience the way my forefathers did, as I constantly remember you in my prayers night and day, longing to see you, even as I recall your tears, so that I may be filled with joy. For I am mindful of the sincere faith within you, which first dwelt in your grandmother Lois and your mother Eunice, and I am sure that it is in you as well. For this reason I remind you to kindle afresh the gift of God which is in you through the laying on of my hands. For God has not given us a spirit of timidity, but of power and love and discipline. (2 Tim. 1:2–7)

Paul understood that the Lord was taking excellent care of Timothy; however, his love and concern for the young pastor of the Ephesian church drove him to his knees. Yet even as he was praying for Timothy to be strengthened, Paul himself was drawn closer to God and was empowered to remain brave in the face of his impending execution.

In the final few sentences of the last epistle he would ever write, Paul testified, "The Lord will rescue me from every evil deed, and will bring me safely to His heavenly kingdom; to Him be the glory forever and ever. Amen" (2 Tim. 4:18).

What a courageous testimony in the face of death! Remember, anything that motivates us to spend time in the Father's presence is ultimately good. Our intimacy with God—His highest priority for our lives—determines the impact of our lives. Therefore, our concern for others, if lived out in prayer, deepens our dependence on and relationship with the Father.

WHAT DO I SAY?

How do you respond when people ask you to pray for them or the Father gives you a burden to intercede for someone? Do you reply with confidence? Or do you fear your petitions will be inadequate?

In the first chapter of Colossians, the apostle Paul gives us a powerful model for intercession. It can be used to lift anyone up to the Lord, regardless of his or her need, because it comes straight from the Word of God. We can be confident that the Father will answer our requests, and when we ask sincerely and consistently, we are assured that He will also use us to impact those around us in positive, eternal ways.

Paul writes:

We give thanks to God, the Father of our Lord Jesus Christ, praying always for you, since we heard of your faith in Christ Jesus and the love which you have for all the saints. . . .

For this reason also, since the day we heard of it, we have not ceased to pray for you and to ask that you may be *filled with the knowledge of His will* in all spiritual wisdom and understanding, so that you will *walk in a manner worthy of the Lord,* to please Him in all respects, *bearing fruit in every good work* and *increasing in the knowledge of God; strengthened with all power,* according to His glorious might, for the attaining of all steadfastness and patience; *joyously giving thanks to the Father,* who has qualified us to share in the inheritance of the saints in Light. (Col. 1:3–12, emphasis added)

In this passage, the apostle Paul gives us an excellent example of how to intercede according to God's will, especially when we don't know exactly what to pray for someone. You see, it is possible that Paul never visited the church at Colossae and had not met the people there. Nor could he go to them, since he was in prison as he wrote the letter (Col. 4:18). He knew of the church through his friend and faithful coworker in Christ, Epaphras (Col. 1:7). Paul said Epaphras was "Always laboring earnestly for you in his prayers, that you may stand perfect and fully assured in all the will of God" (Col. 4:12).

When word reached Paul that false doctrines had begun to infect the congregation, the apostle took action. After all, he loved his brothers and sisters in Christ and wanted the best for them even if he did not know them by name. However, it was a challenge to him all the same. Unable to assess the situation firsthand, understand the personalities involved, or call out specific prayer requests, Paul was left with few facts but a heavy burden.

SIX KEY PETITIONS

Perhaps you face a situation that is likewise vague. You do not know what the Father intends to do in people's lives, whether they need healing, protection, discipline, or simply comfort.

How can you pray for others without getting in the way of what God desires to do in and through them?

Thankfully, when we don't know the details of a person's circumstances, we can count on the fact that the Lord does. Paul gives us an excellent example of how to intercede in a manner that is general in its appearance but profound in its application. Each request is in perfect line with the Father's will as revealed in His Word; it fits every single need we can have in life; and it is centered on the Great Problem Solver. There is nothing selfish about any part of it, but every word magnifies His glorious name.

Let us examine Paul's six petitions and learn the prayer through which God changes lives.

> *Paul gives us an excellent example of how to intercede in a manner that is general in its appearance but profound in its application.*

1. An Understanding of God's Will

Paul asked that the Colossians would be "filled with the knowledge of His will in all spiritual wisdom and understanding" (Col. 1:9). This first request is foundational to all of our petitions because God desires every person to understand His unique plans for them and see their circumstances from His viewpoint. We can also ask that the Lord give people spiritual wisdom and understanding because they must know how to apply the Father's will to their lives—existing for His purposes rather than their own.

After all, the Lord has specific things for each of us to accomplish. Ephesians 2:10 tells us, "We are His workmanship, created in Christ Jesus for good works, which God prepared beforehand so that we would walk in them." We are each formed with a specific set of abilities, talents, and personality traits to serve Him (Ps. 139:13–16). It is as we embrace the Father's objectives and goals that life becomes meaningful and fulfilling.

When we pray for God's plans to be carried out in a person's life, we know we are requesting the best for him or her.

Asking the Lord to reveal His will is the perfect way to begin our petitions. When we pray for God's plans to be carried out in a person's life, we know we are requesting the best for him or her.

2. A Worthy Walk

As we know, Paul was addressing the church at Colossae—Christians who had faith in Jesus as their Savior. So it was good and right for Paul to pray that they would "walk in a manner worthy of the Lord" (Col. 1:10).

As believers, we are the Father's representatives, or as 2 Corinthians 5:20 teaches, "We are ambassadors for Christ, as though God were making an appeal through us; we beg you on behalf of Christ, be reconciled to God." It is not enough that we simply walk down the Father's path for us; rather, we must also do so in a way that brings honor to His name and helps others to know Him. Our lives testify about the Lord we serve, so we must be obedient to Him and conduct ourselves in a manner consistent with His character.

For those during Paul's time, that meant abiding in the Christian walk and not slipping back into pagan practices. To those we pray for, it signifies being "devoted to one another in brotherly love; giv[ing] preference to one another in honor; not lagging behind in diligence, fervent in spirit, serving the Lord; rejoicing in hope, persevering in tribulation, devoted to prayer, contributing to the needs of the saints, [and] practicing hospitality" (Rom. 12:10–13).

Ask the Father to help the person you're praying for to live in a way that honors His name and is pleasing to Him.

Ask the Father to help the person you're praying for to live in a way that honors His name so that his or her conversation, character, and conduct will be pleasing to Him. He will guide your loved one to the right choices and will work through his or her life to make a difference in the lives of others.

3. Fruitful Work

Paul's third request was that the Colossians would bear "fruit in every good work" (Col. 1:10). As believers, we serve the eternal God, and our lives can and should have an everlasting impact. We have the privilege of investing the time, talents, and skills the Lord has given us for the sake of His kingdom, knowing that whatever we accomplish in obedience to Him will endure forever.

I have seen an excellent example in the many Wycliffe Bible translators I've met throughout the years. Some of them spent decades in remote regions of the world—in dangerous and primitive conditions—translating God's Word for people who often did not even have a written language. By the world's standards, the translators did not achieve wealth, status, or power; none claimed an abundant financial portfolio or extensive properties. But they produced fruit of infinitely greater value—influencing souls and leading them into growing relationships with Jesus Christ. There are people who have eternal life because those translators allowed God to work through them. There is no greater reward than that (Prov. 11:30).

Always focus on producing fruit of infinitely great value—influencing souls and leading them into growing relationships with Jesus Christ.

As Jesus said, "My food is to do the will of Him who sent Me and to accomplish His work. Do you not say, 'There are yet four months, and then comes the harvest'? Behold, I say to you, lift up your eyes and look on the fields, that they are white for harvest. Already he who reaps is receiving wages and is gathering fruit for life eternal; so that he who sows and he who reaps may rejoice together" (John 4:34–36).

Paul understood that the Colossians were tempted to compromise their beliefs in order to be accepted by the community and to advance their own goals. However, they needed to remember what mattered and what would last. As he wrote in 1 Corinthians 3:13–14, "Each man's work will become evident; for the day will show it because it is to be revealed with fire, and the fire itself will test the quality of each man's work. If any man's work which he has built on it remains, he will receive a reward. If any man's work is burned up, he will suffer loss."

In other words, if we expend our energies pursuing earthly ambitions, they will pass away. When we obey God, accomplishing His assignments for us, we are assured that they will continue to produce fruit, even when time is no more (Phil. 1:6).

Likewise, those we care about will sometimes wish to do what is easy—to compromise their values in order to ease pain or achieve worldly goals. We should pray for the Lord to "set eternity in their heart" (Eccl. 3:11), giving them an eternal perspective and priority, so they will submit to whatever He wants to do with their lives and allow Him to use them powerfully in His fruitful work.

4. The Knowledge of God

Fourth, Paul prayed that the Colossians would continue "increasing in the knowledge of God" (Col. 1:10); that they would encounter the Father in profoundly intimate and personal ways. In other words, Paul was asking the Lord to help the Colossians experience the ultimate conversation.

As you and I have seen, a person can comprehend a great deal about God but not really know Him—the Good Shepherd, the Great Problem Solver, *YHWH, Elohim, Adonai,* and our beloved Savior. Our understanding of who He is shapes how we interact with Him, what we communicate to Him, and whether we expect Him to answer us. It is of utmost importance that those we intercede for continue to seek Him and learn His ways. With this in mind, we pray:

Ask the Lord to help them experience the ultimate conversation.

First, we ask the Father to reveal Himself to them through Scripture—that He would illuminate their times of prayer and Bible study with greater recognition of His trustworthy character. The habits, behaviors, and practices that help us interact with the Lord are likewise crucial to those for whom we pray. As we have noted, the best place anyone can begin seeking God is through His Word. The Bible not only familiarizes us with what He says but also how He communicates His will to us. We request the Lord to shed light upon Scripture for them in powerful ways.

Second, we ask the Father to motivate and enable them to apply what they have learned in their times alone with Him. We pray they will be courageous and face the issues that the Holy Spirit surfaces, willing to deal with them as He instructs.

We ask the Lord to help them obey Him, regardless of what He directs them to do. And finally we praise Him— understanding that whatever He commands will ultimately help them grow closer to Him and increase their knowledge of His ways.

5. Powerful, Steadfast, Patient Strength

Paul's fifth request for the Colossians was that they would be "strengthened with all power, according to His glorious might, for the attaining of all steadfastness and patience" (Col. 1:11).

Whenever you and I face trials or challenges, our strength may be drained, we may doubt our qualifications and abilities, and we may take our frustrations out on those closest to us. The same is most likely true for the individuals for whom you're praying. They probably feel weak, inadequate, and discouraged. They need God's enabling strength to help them endure, obey Him despite the obstacles they encounter, and be patient with those around them.

Ask the Father to teach them how to lean on Him, rather than their own capabilities.

Ask the Father to teach them how to lean on Him, rather than their own capabilities. Also, pray that their dependence on the Holy Spirit will increase and that they would trust Him to enable them to do His will. Assuredly, He will "confirm, strengthen and establish" (1 Pet. 5:10) them as they rely upon His unfailing power.

6. *A Heart of Joyful Thanks*

The apostle Paul's final petition was that the Colossians would have the right attitude: "joyously giving thanks to the Father, who has qualified us to share in the inheritance of the saints in Light" (Col. 1:11–12). He asked that even in hardship, they would be grateful for all God had done in their lives, counting the many blessings He had given.

Likewise, we should pray that the people we're burdened for will see the Lord's loving-kindness, even in the midst of adversity, trusting that He will bring good out of their sufferings. As 1 Thessalonians 5:18 instructs, "In everything give thanks; for this is God's will for you in Christ Jesus." The word "everything" is challenging because there will be situations when we do not feel particularly grateful. There are troubles we face that negatively affect every aspect of life, stealing our joy and focus away from the Father.

There have even been times through the years when I've walked onto the platform as the church service began and my mind was somewhere else. I was as prepared mentally and spiritually as I could be to preach the message, but emotionally, I was struggling with some devastating issue.

It was in those moments I experienced something extraordinary. As the orchestra played and the choir and congregation began to sing, my heart would respond to the words of those hymns. Giving thanks changed my focus from the difficulty I was facing to God's awesome character, provision, and love. Suddenly, my problems did not seem so overwhelming.

It is important to pray for the Lord to remain enthroned in their praises (Ps. 22:3)—there is nothing better they can do than give Him thanks in the most difficult circumstances. When they take their eyes off their problems and focus on Him, they will realize He has already given them victory. This will not only encourage them but will give them the hope they need to endure as long as their trials last.

Giving thanks changes our focus from the difficulty we're facing to God's awesome character, provision, and love.

GOD WILL WORK THROUGH YOUR PRAYERS

Do you want your loved ones to have intimate, powerful relationships with the Father? Do you desire for them to serve Him passionately and faithfully? Your prayers can have an incredible influence in their lives. Therefore, lift them up to Him regularly, using Paul's words from Colossians as your pattern, and trust God to work in their lives in a mighty way.

With this in mind, I challenge you to commit to memory the outline below. Pray that the people you are burdened for, your friends, and your loved ones would develop:

- An understanding of God's will (Col. 1:9)
- A worthy walk (Col. 1:10)
- Fruitful work (Col. 1:10)

- The knowledge of God (Col. 1:10)
- Powerful, steadfast, patient strength (Col. 1:11)
- A heart of joyful thanks (Col. 1:11–12)

These petitions don't guarantee that every moment of their lives will be easy. But they can help your loved ones become more Christlike—growing in their patience for others, purifying their desires, and enduring their trials.

Your heavenly Father will be faithful to fulfill His promises. So never question whether your conversations with the Lord on behalf of others matter. They do. The requests in Colossians 1:9–12 all align with God's will and can help the people you're praying for succeed in the battles they fight. You may even impact their lives for eternity.

The Lord you serve "is able to do far more abundantly beyond all that we ask or think" (Eph. 3:20) and may do more through your intercession for others than you could ever dream.

I will never forget the sound of my mother's voice as she called out my name to the Father. She would kneel beside me and pray, "God, please help Charles." I recall how she would ask the Lord to keep me safe, enable me to do my schoolwork, and use me for His kingdom.

My mother didn't have any earthly idea of everything the Father would lead me to do. But when I think about her sweet, simple prayers as she knelt in that modest little room in Dry Fork, Virginia, I am utterly amazed and humbled at how God worked through them. She never imagined that I would have the privilege of preaching the gospel all around the world.

Likewise, you may never know the impact of your prayers. Just remember, the Lord you serve "is able to do far more abundantly beyond all that we ask or think, according to the power that works within us" (Eph. 3:20). He may do more through your intercession for others than you could ever dream.

Keep talking to Him and praying for them.

Father, how grateful we are that we can talk to You about anything, including the needs of our families, friends, coworkers, fellow believers, and acquaintances. We thank You for using even the burdens we have for them for our good and Your glory.

We pray for our brothers and sisters in Christ all around the world who faithfully proclaim the gospel despite terrible persecution. Father, we ask You to keep them safe, encourage them, help them understand Your will for their lives, and show them how to walk in a manner worthy of your name. Please make their work fruitful, increase their knowledge of Your ways, give them strength to endure, and create a heart of joyful thanks within them. May they lead many into growing relationships with You.

(continued on next page)

Father, I also pray for this reader and the prayer burdens this person is experiencing. Fill this dear soul with the knowledge of Your will in all spiritual wisdom and understanding so that this person will walk in a manner worthy of Your name, pleasing You in all respects. I ask for this person's life to be very productive, bearing fruit in every good work for the sake of Your kingdom. Empower this reader to increase daily in the knowledge of Your unfailing character and holy ways. Illuminate this individual's time in Scripture, helping this person to apply Your Word and carry out Your commands. Strengthen this believer with all power, according to Your glorious might, so that this person can be steadfast and patient regardless of what happens. And fill this dear soul with joyous thankfulness for Your great love and provision, Father.

Thank You for qualifying us to share in Your salvation and in the great promise of heaven. We love You and praise You, Lord. In Jesus' name we pray. Amen.

11

∽

THE ANSWER TO
OUR HEARTS' DESIRES

Accepting the Challenge to Wait

No BOOK ABOUT THE ULTIMATE conversation with God would be complete if it didn't address how the Father views the desires, goals, and ambitions of our hearts. After all, our dreams are often our most fervent requests as we talk to Him. They are the aspirations that motivate us, stimulating us to grow and achieve. They can drive us to our knees because we long for them so intensely.

It is essential that we know whether the Lord truly cares about the hopes that are vital to us.

Before we examine what God's Word says about this, let me ask you: What is it that you yearn for above everything else in the world? What is the supreme desire of your heart? You probably know what it is because it instantly comes to mind. Perhaps you've asked the Father to provide it for you repeatedly but have yet to see it come to fruition. As the years go by, you may wonder if He will ever answer your particular request.

Most of us have dreams that we long to see fulfilled. We quote the Lord's wonderful promises and wait expectantly for the day when He will reward our faith. Perhaps there are things we want to accomplish, attain, or possess. Whether it's goals that we love to talk about or longings that are so personal we just don't feel comfortable sharing them with others, they are always on our minds whenever we kneel to pray. If the Lord told us He would give us anything we wanted, we know exactly what it would be.

Our dreams inspire and motivate us, stimulating us to grow and achieve.

There's nothing wrong with this. We see throughout Scripture that God Himself has desires, such as His wish "for all to come to repentance" (2 Pet. 3:9). Our Creator designed us with the capacity to plan and pursue objectives because they inspire us to persevere in spite of adversity. He also plants dreams within all believers in order to bless us and motivate us to seek Him.

THE DETERMINATION TO DRIVE

When my daughter, Becky, turned sixteen, she let me know that one of her goals was to own a car. Of course, she had other objectives, such as finishing high school, going to college, having a family, and so forth. She was a bright young lady with a wonderful future ahead of her, and I trusted her implicitly. But at that point, I wasn't ready for her to have an automobile, and she understood my reasons. My decision, however, did not diminish her desire for her own means of transportation. So she spent the next two years praying for God's will.

Our Creator designed us with the capacity to plan and pursue objectives because they inspire us to persevere in spite of adversity and motivate us to seek Him.

At age eighteen, Becky came to me and said, "I've been praying and asking the Lord about my car. Here is what I think God wants me to get." She then proceeded to describe the automobile in detail—the year, model, color, and features that vehicle was going to have. She had it all settled, which made me chuckle.

I replied, "Keep talking to the Lord about it. Whatever He says is fine with me."

Several months went by, and she continued to seek the Father's will. She never said a word; she just kept praying and trusting the Lord would answer her.

One night we were having dinner and chatting as we always did, and my son, Andy, said, "Becky, you've been praying about getting a car, haven't you? Maybe we should look at the newspaper and see if we can find what you want." It seemed like a good idea. After dinner, we opened the "For Sale" section of the local paper and began reading.

Wouldn't you know it—there was an ad for an automobile

just like the one Becky had been dreaming about. Andy immediately called the owner, and we went over to his place to take a look. Sure enough, the car was everything Becky wanted. The price was right, and before long, it was hers.

The reason I tell you this story is because God does care about your desires, and there is absolutely nothing wrong with having them. Jesus tells us, "I say to you, if you ask the Father for anything *in My name,* He will give it to you" (John 16:23, emphasis added). That doesn't mean we should expect the Lord to give us whatever we want, whenever we want it. The key is *asking in His name,* or in line with His will.

Although Becky wanted a car, she sought the kind that God wanted her to have and waited for Him to lead the way to it. She put the Lord first, even in this simple request, because she understood that when our dreams align with the Father's purpose and plan for our lives, we are assured that He will fulfill them.

> *The question we should always ask is:* Do my desires fit God's purpose and plan for my life?

As 1 John 5:14–15 (emphasis added) confirms, "This is the confidence which we have before Him, that, if we ask *anything according to His will*, He hears us. And if we know that He hears us in whatever we ask, we know that we have the requests which we have asked from Him."

This is why the question you and I should always ask whenever considering our goals, dreams, and aspirations is: *Do my desires fit God's purpose and plan for my life?*

MY DESIRES OR HIS?

Perhaps you are wondering if your most cherished wish is the Lord's will for you. Maybe you're uncertain whether He inspired the yearning in your heart at this very moment. And if it is not from Him, will you be forced to give it up?

That depends on the nature of your aspirations—and this is where you need to be cautious. If you understand who God is, you automatically know that there are some habits and behaviors that are inconsistent with His character.

For example, 1 Timothy 6:9–10 tells us, "Those who want to get rich fall into temptation and a snare and many foolish and harmful desires which plunge men into ruin and destruction. For the love of money is a root of all sorts of evil, and some by longing for it have wandered away from the faith and pierced themselves with many griefs."

The Father will not honor your sinful cravings because He knows they lead to emptiness, pain, suffering, and disappointment. They can even result in devastation and death (Prov. 14:12). That is not the future He wants for you. However, if you persist in demanding your own way and seeking to gratify your fleshly longings, He may allow you to get what you want and face the consequences (Rom. 1:24).

You must be careful with what you wish to attain. In order to discern whether the desire of your heart fits His purpose for your life, you must seek His guidance. Be assured: The Father will move heaven and earth to show you His will, and He always provides His best for you. You can be confident that if something you want doesn't fit His awesome plan for you, He will reveal His opposition to it when you seek Him.

Many times you can do this simple test: If what you seek causes you to leave God out of your life or hinders your relationship with Him, then it doesn't originate with the Lord. If your desires tempt you to run from the Father or toward sin, then they don't come from Him.

If what you seek hinders your relationship with God, then you can be certain it doesn't originate with Him.

On the other hand, a righteous longing not only draws us closer to the Father; it is also His gift to us. We know this from His awesome promise in Psalm 37:4, "Delight yourself in the LORD; and He will give you the desires of your heart." Our responsibility is to seek Him wholeheartedly and obey His commands. When we do, He blesses us by giving us praiseworthy yearnings, and then He satisfies them in a manner beyond our imaginations.

OUR RESPONSIBILITY

Once we know that a dream or goal is from the Father, how do we anticipate it in a way that honors Him as time passes? After all, it's easy to keep the faith when we don't have to wait too long for God to bless us. That's not usually the case. The stronger our desires, the more quickly our patience tends to fall short. As the days, weeks, and months go by, we may find it increasingly difficult to trust that He will answer our prayers. We may begin to doubt that the Lord will ever satisfy our longings.

That may be where you find yourself today. If your desire is truly from God, why has He delayed in fulfilling His promises to you? And how do you maintain your trust in the Lord until He brings it to fruition? To answer this, we need to look at the context of the Father's promise in Psalm 37:4–7. David writes:

> Delight yourself in the LORD;
> And He will give you the desires of your heart.
> Commit your way to the LORD,
> Trust also in Him, and He will do it.
> He will bring forth your righteousness as the light
> And your judgment as the noonday.
> Rest in the LORD and wait patiently for Him;
> Do not fret because of him who prospers in his way,
> Because of the man who carries out wicked schemes.

1. Make the Lord Our Delight

In this passage, we see that God's pledge to us comes with an important responsibility. Yes, He will grant us the desires of our hearts, but we must first delight ourselves in Him. How do we do this? By seeking, obeying, and pleasing Him, and by rejoicing that He is our Lord and Savior. When we focus on

God and feel the joy of His presence, we tend to stop arguing with Him about what is best for our lives.

When I was very young, my mother taught me that where our mind goes, our feet are soon to follow. If our minds are always trained upon what we're yearning for, we will undoubtedly struggle with impatience. If we keep our attention fixed on the Lord, we will be able to endure victoriously. As Isaiah 26:3 tells us, "The steadfast of mind You will keep in perfect peace, because he trusts in You."

> *If we keep our attention fixed on the Lord, we will be able to endure victoriously.*

This is what the Father wants—what delighting in Him really means. We focus on Him completely, to the point where His plans and purposes become our own.

2. Commit Our Ways to God

Second, Psalm 37:5 instructs, "Commit your way to the LORD, trust also in Him, and He will do it." We must be so dedicated to doing God's will that we are willing to lay down our desires if He asks us to. In other words, we should be more devoted to Him than to our own hopes and dreams.

This takes faith because we can commit only to Someone we absolutely trust. One of the reasons we may fail to obey the Lord is a lack of confidence that He has our best interests at heart.

Romans 8:31–32 assures us, "If God is for us, who is against us? He who did not spare His own Son, but delivered Him over for us all, how will He not also with Him freely give us all things?" The Father is merciful, kind, and generous. He understands our personalities, skills, and hidden longings. The Lord also knows what the future holds.

You and I can trust our heavenly Father with our hopes and dreams because He knows what we desire and what will satisfy our souls. He is worthy of our confidence. He will not settle for anything less than His best for us, and neither should we. If we have faith in Him, He will accomplish it for us.

> *You and I can trust our heavenly Father with our hopes and dreams because He knows what we desire and what will satisfy our souls.*

3. Rest and Wait for the Father

Finally, Psalm 37:7 tells us, "Rest in the LORD and wait patiently for Him." When we murmur, fret, and complain, we are not demonstrating trust; we're arguing with God. That doesn't speed up the process at all; on the contrary, it hinders His work and our growth.

Rather, to rest in the Father means that we lean on His provision. We trust Him to answer our prayers in His timing and to transform our dreams so they conform to His will. Of course, this also means we have to let go of our agendas and wait for the Father, which usually stretches our faith in Him. Waiting is one of the most difficult things we will ever do as

Christians. But we must realize that while we are patiently expecting the Lord's answer, He is actively engaged on our behalf: arranging our circumstances, purifying our motives, teaching us to rely on Him, protecting us from unseen dangers, and preparing us to influence others.

When I was just a lad, my mother taught me this principle through a wonderful lesson about gardening. I can still remember how we went out to the backyard and she prepared a small, three-foot-square area so we could sow some seeds. Even though I had no idea what we were growing, I was very eager to see what would happen.

We dug some holes, planted those seeds in the ground, and covered them up again. Then Mother explained that it wouldn't be long before we noticed tiny green sprouts coming up, which would confirm that something was developing below the soil. Not long after that, we would have fruit. So day after day, I would walk out to the backyard and look for evidence of growth. Seeing none, I began to grow impatient. And after a week, I was so frustrated that I decided to find out what was happening with those seeds.

So I dug them up.

I did not realize that it was going to take a while for the plants to mature and produce fruit. And because of my haste to see results, I destroyed those seeds right as they were developing. How much fruit did I grow? None.

That experience taught me a lesson about being patient and waiting for God's timing. Every day He arranges the circumstances of our lives and works to bring us into intimate relationships with Himself. Even when we cannot see His activity, He is drawing us closer, teaching us His ways, and fulfilling His promises to us. The Lord has a schedule for how He will answer our prayers and help each of us progress spiritually, conforming us to the image of Christ. However, we should not allow ourselves to become impatient or try to take control because there are destructive consequences to our actions.

The Father admonishes us in Psalm 46:10 to "Cease striving and know that I am God." It's never up to us to figure out how we will lay hold of His promises or to speed the process along. We must stop thinking that we can achieve His goals for us in our own strength and realize that the One who created the heavens and the earth has our lives in His hands. Our responsibility is simple—to rest in eager anticipation of His provision for us and to trust: "The Lord will accomplish what concerns me" (Ps. 138:8).

> *"Keep traveling steadily along His pathway and in due season He will honor you with every blessing."*
> *(Ps. 37:34 TLB)*

God works on behalf of those who wait for Him (Isa. 64:4). As Psalm 37:34 (TLB) admonishes, "Don't be impatient for the Lord to act! Keep traveling steadily along His pathway and in due season He will honor you with every blessing."

ENDURING UNTIL HIS ANSWER COMES

What is it that you hope for above everything else in the world? As we've discussed, your desires are an important part of your Christian walk. Your godly dreams motivate you to fulfill the Father's plans for you. They encourage you to press on toward your goals, despite hardships. And they inspire you to seek His face.

How do you continue delighting yourself in Him, committing your ways to Him, and patiently anticipating His provision as you wait for His blessing? How can you avoid fretting, becoming impatient, losing your faith, or running ahead of Him? How do you trust Him for His best today and every day, knowing that if you remain faithful, He will satisfy the desires of your heart?

1. Seek God with Perseverance

First, you must persevere in the ultimate conversation with God—*continuing firmly on course in spite of any obstacle or difficulties.* Don't give up. Rather, remain in steadfast, constant communion with the Father, focusing on Him rather than your circumstances.

Jesus said, "Ask, and it will be given to you; seek, and you will find; knock, and it will be opened to you. For everyone who asks receives, and he who seeks finds, and to him who knocks it will be opened" (Matt. 7:7–8). The Savior invites us to approach the Father freely with our petitions and expect Him to provide all we need.

Jesus never promised that every door would open immediately. On the contrary, in telling us to "seek" and "knock," Jesus used a Greek verb form called the *present imperative*. These two verbs are best translated as "knock, and keep on knocking" and "seek, and keep on seeking." In other words, perseverance is a vital aspect of answered prayer. Some of the gifts the Father has for us can come only after long seasons of waiting and praying.

Therefore, do not be discouraged if you don't achieve your goals or receive the desires of your heart when you think you should. The Lord knows exactly what you need—what graces must be developed in your character, what changes ought to be made in your life, what areas in your faith require growth, and what details should be arranged. He will wait until you are ready.

> *Some of the gifts the Father has for us can come only after long seasons of waiting and praying.*

For example, the desire of David's heart was to be king of Israel, in obedience to God's command (1 Sam. 16:12–13). But the time from when Samuel anointed him as the successor to Saul until David ruled the entire nation (2 Sam. 5:1–5) was more than *two decades*! And it was very difficult for him. At one point he wrote, "I am weary with my crying; my throat is parched; my eyes fail while I wait for my God" (Ps. 69:3).

Perhaps you've felt the same way while waiting for your dreams to become a reality. It is easy to become discouraged and lose hope if your focus isn't on the Father.

Thankfully, David had his eyes fixed on the Lord. At the end of his life, he testified,

> As for God, His way is blameless;
> The word of the LORD is tested;
> He is a shield to all who take refuge in Him.
> For who is God, besides the LORD?
> And who is a rock, besides our God?
> God is my strong fortress;
> And He sets the blameless in His way.
> He makes my feet like hinds' feet,
> And sets me on my high places.
> He trains my hands for battle,
> So that my arms can bend a bow of bronze.
> You have also given me the shield of Your salvation,
> And Your help makes me great. (2 Sam. 22:31–36)

David understood that it was God who had trained him to be king and established him on the throne of Israel. He saw firsthand that it is always worthwhile to wait upon the Father. You will as well. So give the Lord the time to accomplish His will in your life. Don't give up; just keep obeying Him.

2. Seek God with Confidence

Second, we are to pray with *confidence—with belief in the trustworthiness of the Lord.* We are completely convinced that He will do as He says.

Jesus said, "What man is there among you who, when his son asks for a loaf, will give him a stone? Or if he asks for a fish, he will not give him a snake, will he? If you then, being evil, know how to give good gifts to your children, *how much more* will your Father who is in heaven give what is good to those who ask Him!" (Matt. 7:9–11, emphasis added).

We should pay attention to what Jesus is saying here. The stones around the Sea of Galilee were round, the same color and shape of their daily bread. They appeared right but were in no way the same. No parent would knowingly give stones to his or her child. Likewise, the snakes probably looked like fish that could be caught there. However, they were not only poisonous; finless fish such as eels were prohibited by Levitical law (Lev. 11:1, 9–12). No good mother or father would allow his or her little one to eat such a creature.

> *How much more will our heavenly Father—our holy, righteous, loving God—give when we ask Him to lead us?*

With this in mind, how much more will our heavenly Father—our holy, righteous, loving God—give when we ask Him to lead us?

In other words, there are things in life that *seem to be* what you and I may want. Perhaps there is a certain person you want to marry or a job you wish the Lord would give you. But God knows when what you desire is not what will satisfy you. You believe you are getting a loaf of bread or a fish that will nourish you, fill you up, and give you energy. But the Lord sees more deeply than you do. He knows whether that individual or position you've been praying about will turn out to be like a rock or a poisonous snake to your system—devastating.

You can rest assured that God will divert you from danger as long as you are listening to Him. Your perfect, loving, heavenly Father waits to give you exactly what you need because He cares for you. He can be trusted to give you gifts that are beneficial in every way. Therefore, seek Him *confidently,* knowing He will never steer you wrong or fail to keep His promise to you. Don't move ahead without Him.

MORE THAN WE CAN IMAGINE

As I've recounted in this book, the desire of my heart throughout my life has been to serve God and lead people into growing relationships with Jesus Christ. My desire began in 1947, when I was fourteen and the Lord called me to preach the gospel. There were many times when, from a human standpoint, it looked like the Father would not fulfill my dream to tell people about Him because I lacked money, faced opposition, and encountered other obstacles. However, time after time, He proved Himself faithful in giving me everything I needed to serve Him.

In 1971 God allowed me to become pastor of First Baptist Church in Atlanta. I remember praying at that point that we could take the message of salvation outside the walls of the church. Soon thereafter, the Lord provided the opportunity for us to broadcast a simple thirty-minute program called *The Chapel Hour* on WXIA-TV 11 and WANX 46. Then TBS on Channel 17 gave us a time slot to preach the gospel. Afterward, the Christian Broadcasting Network called and asked to use some of our sermon tapes. We kept listening to and trusting God, and doors kept opening. In 1980 our first radio broadcast began airing on a small 100,000-watt border station in McAllen, Texas—KVMV-FM 96.9.

I could not believe all the Father was doing. The ministry was growing, and In Touch Ministries was adding television and radio stations constantly. It was astounding.

Then God started stirring something within me. I recall reading Psalm 67:2 (TLB), which says, "Send us around the world with the news of Your saving power and your eternal plan for all mankind." That got ahold of me. I wondered whether the Lord wanted me to go into the mission field, so I told Him I would do whatever He asked.

> *"Send us around the world with the news of Your saving power and your eternal plan for all mankind."*
> (Ps. 67:2 TLB)

At other times, I would read the Great Commission, which says, "Go therefore and make disciples of all the nations, baptizing them in the name of the Father and the Son and the

Holy Spirit, teaching them to observe all that I commanded you; and lo, I am with you always, even to the end of the age" (Matt. 28:19–20). I would get stuck at the part that said: "Make disciples *of all the nations.*"

The truth was, I longed to see people saved, and we were doing a good job of that here in the United States. But it wasn't enough. I realized that what I wanted was to take the gospel all around the world. I began to pray about it.

One particular morning, God spoke to me powerfully. It was the late eighties, and In Touch was having a rally in Kansas City. I was on my knees before the Father, reading His Word and asking for His guidance on the message I was to preach. When I was done, I got up and looked out the large bay window at the coliseum where our rally would be. Just outside was a building with nothing but satellite dishes and broadcast antennas crowded on its roof. In that moment, I felt as if the Lord said, "That's the way I'm going to do it. That is how I will use you to send the gospel around the world."

I never said a word to anyone about it. I just watched God work everything out in an amazing way. Now, more than two decades later, not only have our broadcast messages been translated into more than one hundred dialects, we are also on television and radio stations around the world, preaching the good news of salvation. We have websites in languages such as Mandarin, Hindi, Farsi, and Korean. Our solar-powered In Touch *Messengers*—which include thirty-five sermons teaching the truth of the gospel—are now in twelve languages, with more in development.

I believe we are living in the most exciting, most cutting-edge time in the history of the world, able to tell so many people in so many different countries about Jesus. We did not plan any of it. God has opened every door. We simply obeyed Him and were blessed in return.

I say all this so that you will be encouraged. No matter what obstacles there are to your heart's desire, do not give up hope. Regardless of how long you must wait, keep trusting and obeying the Lord with perseverance and confidence. If your dream is from the Father, you can be certain He will bring it to pass.

> *We did not plan any of it. God has opened every door. We simply obeyed Him and were blessed in return.*

He has great and wonderful plans for your life, more awesome than you could ever imagine (Eph. 3:20–21). Stay in this ultimate conversation with Him, make Him your delight, commit your way to Him, and rest in His loving care. And never forget to "hold fast the confession of [y]our hope without wavering, for He who promised is faithful" (Heb. 10:23).

Father, how grateful we are that You love us the way You do. You care for us just as we are and always provide the very best for Your children. Lord, please give us the wisdom to discern

(continued on next page)

Your plans and purposes for our lives. When our desires are a hindrance to our relationships with You, please reveal them so we can repent of them.

Lord God, I pray specifically for this reader today, that You will reveal Your wonderful hopes and dreams to his or her waiting heart. Give this dear soul the confidence to persevere in faith, regardless of the obstacles and challenges that arise. Show this individual how to delight in You, commit to Your will, rest in Your ways, and wait for perfect timing. Thank You for Your awesome plans for this person's life.

To You be all the wisdom, glory, power, and praise, Lord God Almighty. In the wonderful and matchless name of Jesus, I pray. Amen.

12

⌒

INTIMACY WITH GOD

Peace and Joy in His Presence Forever

THERE ARE MANY DAYS WHEN I cannot wait to get home and be alone with the Father. I am eager to leave behind all the stresses and decisions, change out of my suit and tie, go into my prayer closet, open God's Word, and relax in His loving arms. Many times I don't need to say a word, I simply want to hear from the Lord, experiencing His peaceful wisdom and loving presence. There is nothing better in life than just being with Him.

That is what the ultimate conversation is all about—*intimacy with God*. We fellowship with the Father, learn His ways, and enjoy His company. We walk with Him through the mountains and valleys of life, always trusting that He will lead us in the best way possible. As we do, He reproduces His life in us, conforming us to His character and filling us with His joy.

Is this what you desire? Wouldn't you like to hear the Father say to you, "My child, I love you and have everything under control. I am going to guide you through each diffi-

culty. I will strengthen and empower you through every circumstance. I'll work through whatever situation you face in
order to reveal Myself to you and trans-
form the lives of others." Do you long to
hear Him say that to you personally? Well,
then, be comforted—this is the message
that He gives you throughout Scripture
(Gen. 28:15; Deut. 31:6, 8; Isa. 41:10;
Jer. 1:8, 19; 15:20; Matt. 28:20). It is also
what He wants you to hide in your heart
today.

> *That is what the ultimate conversation is all about*—intimacy with God.

Friend, God *wants you to know Him*. He would love for you
to sit quietly in His presence and say, "Lord, today I don't desire anything but You. I hunger to know You better and understand You more. I long for a deeper relationship with You
and to give myself to You fully." Intimacy with the Father is
more than what you and I can do to make Him happy or what
He does in answer to our prayers.

Intimacy says, "God, here is my heart. I am willing to be
vulnerable before You in every way—in my soul, my spirit,
and everything I am. I am holding absolutely nothing back."
The relationship is intensely *personal* and *profound*. It is about
who we are—our personalities, characters, skills, and everything else about us—being devoted to who He is, just as He
is to us.

Think about the amazing invitation He has given you.
The most powerful thing you can do—the most awesome
privilege you have in this life—is to talk to the heavenly Fa-

ther about anything in your heart. You can touch anyone, anywhere in the world, through your prayers, no matter the circumstance. You can move mountains, change nations, and overcome any problem as you talk with the Lord. And you will know Him "fully just as [you] also have been fully known" (1 Cor. 13:12).

I pray that you will know the Father in this way and that you will be motivated to entrust Him with every area of your life because there is nothing so beneficial or freeing as experiencing an intimate relationship with God. When you open yourself completely to His unfailing love, He builds within you *stability, security, spiritual understanding, sensitivity,* and *serenity.*

The most powerful thing you can do—the most awesome privilege you have in this life—is to talk to the heavenly Father about anything in your heart.

First, intimacy with the Lord builds *stability* in your life. A relationship with God is like an anchor that keeps you grounded, no matter the circumstances, because He never changes; His character is unfailingly trustworthy. Although people and situations come and go, He remains the same omnipotent, omniscient, omnipresent, omni-benevolent Lord who will never leave or forsake you (Deut. 31:6, 8).

Not only can you be confident that God has the *ability* to help you, you can be assured that He is genuinely *willing* to listen to you and come to your aid. The combination assures us a life of steadfast stability.

Second, as you grow in your relationship with the Savior,

you realize how *secure* you are in Him. As you learn to hear the Lord's voice, He will teach you how profoundly He cares for you just as you are—not because you are perfect but because it is His nature as your Good Shepherd to do so. As 1 John 4:10 teaches us, "In this is love, not that we loved God, but that He loved us and sent His Son to be the propitiation for our sins." Our duty is not to succeed; that is His responsibility. Rather, our job is to trust in His love and respond to His call in faith and obedience.

> *Our duty is not to succeed; that is His responsibility. Rather, our job is to trust in His love and respond to His call in faith and obedience.*

Your heavenly Father communicates with you personally about His wise provision and protection in preparation for all that is ahead. You can have unquestioning confidence in His leadership.

Third, spending time daily in the ultimate conversation with God—listening to Him in prayer and meditating upon Scripture—will increase your *spiritual understanding.* As you interact with the Father, you begin to comprehend His Word in deeper ways than ever before, and He allows you to see your circumstances from His perspective (Jer. 33:3).

Always remember, the Lord is *constantly* teaching you, patiently demonstrating His love and wisdom to you through every event and detail of your life. You may be amazed by how much more you are able to understand about the world around you as you grow in your knowledge of His ways.

Therefore, seek the Father privately, humbly, sincerely, and obediently, for He loves and accepts you just as you are. Focus on His authority, holiness, power, wisdom, purpose, provision, forgiveness, and goodness. And listen closely to the promptings of His Spirit.

When you engage in this constant, intimate communication with the Father in a real and living way, you begin to know and understand things that are apparent only to those who understand the deep truths of His Holy Spirit. As you experience more of the Father's faultless character in your life, you will grow more confident in His provision for you, regardless of your circumstances or the obstacles you encounter.

> *Your intimacy with God determines the impact—the power and influence—of your life on those around you.*

Fourth, intimacy with the Father will allow you to develop *sensitivity* toward others, understanding the struggles they experience. The ultimate conversation makes you far more effective as you relate to and minister to others, since your intimacy with God determines the impact—the power and influence—of your life on those around you. He increases your understanding of certain types of suffering so you will be a better minister of the gospel. Second Corinthians 1:3–7 (emphasis added) explains:

Blessed be the God and Father of our Lord Jesus Christ, the Father of mercies and God of all comfort, *who comforts us in all our affliction so that we will be able to comfort those who are in any affliction with the comfort with which we ourselves are comforted by God.* For just as the sufferings of Christ are ours in abundance, so also our comfort is abundant through Christ. But *if we are afflicted, it is for your comfort and salvation; or if we are comforted, it is for your comfort,* which is effective in the patient enduring of the same sufferings which we also suffer; and our hope for you is firmly grounded, *knowing that as you are sharers of our sufferings, so also you are sharers of our comfort.*

Thanks to the work of the Holy Spirit in you, you become more responsive to the needs and emotions of other people. You teach them what the Father showed you during your times of hardship and trial. You are able to offer them meaningful counsel and encouragement that enables them to endure.

> *Everything reaching your life is permitted by Your holy, loving Father, and your situation is in His capable hands.*

Finally, your continuing conversation with the Lord is the key to *serenity.* Another way I often say that is: *Peace with God is the fruit of oneness with Him.* Even in difficult times or when awaiting the fulfillment of your heart's desires, your spirit is calm and tranquil. You are confident that everything reaching your life is permitted by your holy, loving Father, and your situation is in His capable hands.

Each time you face a challenge or time of suffering, you will look forward to the increasingly profound and meaningful ways He will reveal Himself to you because you trust the promise of Romans 8:28: "God causes all things to work together for good to those who love God, to those who are called according to *His* purpose."

The better you know the Lord's spotless character, the less you will ask for, because you have faith in His perfect plan and unfailing provision. And the more you leave your circumstances in His hands and obey Him, the more He will give you.

Opening yourself to an intimate relationship with the Father can seem daunting, but I can assure you, there is nothing in the world more worthwhile or wonderful than knowing Him and experiencing His love. You'll find that as you increasingly devote yourself to God, your desire to be in His presence will grow as well.

Consider the last time you said, "Lord, I want to know You. I don't desire anything but You. I long for a deeper relationship with You. Teach me, guide me, and lead me today. Speak to my heart. I love You and surrender my life to You."

The Sovereign of the universe has all power to meet your every need, to answer your prayers and give you direction. God is willing to speak if you're willing to listen. Engage in the ultimate conversation with Him, trust His unfailing care, and allow Him to pour His unconditional love into your heart, because that is life at its very best.

Father, how grateful we are that You—perfect, holy, awesome God—desire to enter into relationship with us and communicate with us in such powerful ways. Thank You for reconciling us to Yourself through the death and resurrection of Your Son, Jesus Christ. You have given us the most wonderful gift, Lord—an amazing opportunity to be able to interact, fellowship, and develop intimacy with You. Thank You for the ultimate conversation; for the daily privilege of walking with You. We are so grateful that You teach us how to listen to You and enable us to do Your will.

Father, I pray especially for this reader who desires to communicate with You and know You better. Lord God, draw this dear person into an intimate relationship with You daily, teaching this individual how to connect with You in deeper, more meaningful ways than ever before. I ask that You strengthen and fill him or her with faith through Your Spirit. May this person be rooted and grounded in Your love and able to comprehend with all the saints what is the breadth, length, height, and depth of the love of Jesus in a manner that surpasses knowledge. And may Christ work through this dear soul in a powerful way to influence all those around him or her.

Help Your child walk with You daily in the ultimate conversation and be open, yielded, and available for whatever You desire to do. I am grateful that You will reveal Your ways and make Yourself known to this precious soul.

To You be all the honor, glory, power, and praise now and forever, Father. For truly, You are worthy of our service, our lives, and our wholehearted devotion. We love You and thank You for loving us. In Jesus' matchless name, I pray. Amen.

Have a "quiet time" moment.

Subscribe to the In Touch daily devotional email.

intouch.org/subscriptions

God bless our prayer warriors.

in the Impact Prayer Team to receive prayer requests about In Touch
nistry initiatives, encouraging messages, and the blessings
a fruitful prayer life.

:ouch.org/prayerteam

In Touch
Impact Prayer
T · E · A · M

HOWARD READING GROUP GUIDE

Prayer: The Ultimate Conversation
Charles F. Stanley

INTRODUCTION

Prayer means talking to God, right? But it also includes listening for His response. Prayer is a two-way conversation between you and the Father. Whether you're new to the practice of prayer or a seasoned believer looking to deepen and enrich your communion with the Lord, *Prayer: The Ultimate Conversation,* by pastor and teacher Dr. Charles Stanley, is a clear, concise, and practical guide to developing a closer relationship with God.

FOR DISCUSSION

1. If someone asked you, "What is prayer?" how would you describe it? What is prayer's purpose?

2. Have you ever thought of prayer as a two-way conversation between you and God, involving both speaking and listening? Why or why not?

3. Describe the role that prayer currently plays in your life. Are you satisfied with your prayer life? Do you ever wish for deeper and more satisfying communication with God? Explain.

4. Dr. Stanley emphasizes that prayer is a privilege. Do you agree? What is the prerequisite that enables us to have this privilege?

5. What do you suppose God is like? Where have you gotten your ideas about the Lord?

6. Discuss how a person's view of God affects his or her attitude toward prayer.

7. Do your childhood memories affect your prayer life positively or negatively? For example, are you comfortable calling God "Father"?

8. Are you confident that God hears and responds to your prayers? Why or why not?

9. When might prayer be a case of just "talking to yourself"? How can this situation be remedied?

10. What role does the Bible play in prayer? How can we use Scripture to enhance our prayer lives?

11. In addition to the Bible, Dr. Stanley describes some other ways we might hear God speaking to us. What are some of these ways? Have you ever experienced any of them? If someone said to you, "God told me . . . ," what would be your typical reaction?

12. If someone said to you, "I don't need to pray, because God can read my mind," how would you respond to him or her?

13. Dr. Stanley asserts that forgiving others is key to a healthy prayer life and outlines some steps to forgiveness, including focusing on Christ's love and compassion toward us, confessing anger and hurt feelings, and laying aside any desire for retaliation. Are you able to complete these steps? If not, which one is tripping you up? Do you agree that an unforgiving spirit dampens prayer's effectiveness?

14. What is the role of the Holy Spirit in prayer? Have you experienced the Holy Spirit moving in your life?

15. How does your own experience of prayer compare to Dr. Stanley's? Has reading *Prayer: The Ultimate Conversation* inspired any new insights or changes to the way you pray?

A Conversation with Dr. Charles Stanley

Can you discuss the title, *Prayer: The Ultimate Conversation*, and how it relates to the central message of your book?

The ultimate conversation is that lifelong, daily, intimate relationship with God that you and I have been invited to enjoy. I believe that there is nothing in the world more worthwhile, more fulfilling, or more energizing than knowing Him and being in His presence. I wish everyone could experience this, which is why I wrote this book. I hope to help others understand how to enjoy fellowship with God and experience the blessings He has for each of us.

What factor(s) inspired you to write *Prayer: The Ultimate Conversation*? Do you think it is an especially timely message for today's Christians?

I do think it is a timely message. People ask me all the time "How do I pray?" Or "How can I know God better?" *Prayer: The Ultimate Conversation* is an answer to those questions.

I was inspired to write this book in part because this year marks my eightieth birthday and fifty-fifth year in ministry. We are also celebrating In Touch's thirty-fifth anniversary. And as I think back over my life and all the things that have been accomplished, I know I owe it all to God's guidance and provision.

I could never have dreamed where He would lead me or what He would do. So *Prayer: The Ultimate Conversation* is also a testimony of the Father's love and faithfulness. I am so thankful for what He has done in my life and what He will continue to do in eternity.

What do you find are the two or three most common reasons that people experience an unsatisfactory prayer life?

First, I think a person's view of prayer has a great deal to do with whether he or she finds it satisfying or not. If a person is seeking the Father only during emergencies or to give Him a list of requests, he or she is not going to experience the same profound joy and benefits as someone who spends time in His presence to know Him and learn His ways.

Second, how a person sees God can impact his or her prayer life. If an individual does not have an accurate view of the Father's abilities and character, he or she may not feel that it is a valuable practice. But once you know the omnipotent, omniscient, omnipresent loving Lord of all creation, you know that time with Him is absolutely priceless.

Third, how a person applies what he or she hears from God makes a tremendous difference. Some people are passive listeners. They may pray, but they don't really expect the Lord to answer or put what they learn from Him into practice. That's never going to be satisfying. If we desire a truly fulfilling prayer life we must anticipate the Father's response and apply His instruction.

When people pray and listen for a response from God, is there a danger that they will mistake their own thoughts

and desires for God's wisdom and guidance? How can this be avoided?

Yes, any of us can fall into this trap—especially if there is something we really want. We can be so motivated to pursue a particular goal or course of action that we fail to truly hear God's direction.

This is why I always pray with the Bible open in front of me. God will never tell you or me to do anything that contradicts His Word. Therefore it is always important to measure everything we do against Scripture.

What does the apostle Paul mean when he tells Christians to "pray without ceasing" (1 Thessalonians 5:17)? Is it ever possible to overpray? Is there a time when it's appropriate to stop praying and start doing?

The apostle Paul believed, as do I, that we can live in constant conversation with the Father, even as we go about our daily routines. God is interested in every aspect of our lives, and He invites us to talk to Him about everything we face. Does this mean we are always on our knees before Him or continuously uttering prayers? No. Rather, it means that He is in the forefront of our thoughts at all times, and we should consistently listen for His direction. We should go to God first whether we are making a decision, need help, or simply require some encouragement.

So, does there come a time when we should stop praying? Yes and no. Certainly we see that God tells the prophet

Jeremiah, "Do not pray for this people, and do not lift up a cry or prayer for them, and do not intercede with Me" (Jeremiah 7:16). The Lord had decided how He was going to deal with the nation of Judah's disobedience, and there was no way Jeremiah was going to talk Him out of it. Likewise, when God shows you His will, it is time for obedience and action—not more deliberation.

However, even though the Father told Jeremiah to stop praying on behalf of Judah, it did not mean the prophet could no longer talk to the Lord about anything else. In fact, when we step out in obedience to God, that is when it is most crucial for us to remain in continual communication with Him because that is when we are most vulnerable to our doubts and fears. Therefore, we may need to stop praying about certain topics, but we should never give up interacting with the Father.

If readers take away one primary message from *Prayer: The Ultimate Conversation,* what do you hope it will be?

That life at its very best is possible through an intimate relationship with God. The Father loves us and wants us to know Him. And when we seek Him, not only will He reveal Himself to us but will lead us in ways that astound us—filling us with joy, power, and purpose.

What other books or projects are you working on?

As I said, we are commemorating our thirty-fifth anniversary this year at In Touch Ministries, so I have been focused on celebrating all the Lord has done and have also been actively seeking His guidance for what is ahead for the ministry.

He's led us to take on two special projects that I am very excited about. We have never done anything like them. The first is a book of quotations from my "Life Principles to Live By" sermon series. It is called *Walking with God* and it covers a wide spectrum of topics on the Christian life. I pray it will encourage and bless those who read it.

The second book is one that I've dreamed about for a very long time. It is entitled *I Love to Tell the Story* and it contains many of the photographs I have been blessed to take over the years. Truly, we can see the wisdom, splendor, and sovereignty of the Father in every part of His creation, and it has been an honor to serve Him and worship Him through photography.

There is much more, of course, and I am thankful to be walking in my own ultimate conversation with the Father that grows and deepens daily. He fills every day with hope and joyful anticipation. I am so grateful for everything He has done. And so I will continue obeying God and leaving all the consequences to Him. Because He has absolutely awesome things planned for the future—and, friend, I don't want to miss any of them!

Enhance Your Book Club

1. Begin or end each meeting in prayer for each other. Try to keep the principles of *Prayer: The Ultimate Conversation* in mind as you pray. What effect does it have on your meeting?

2. As a group watch Dr. Stanley's video "How Can I Pray Effectively?" at www.intouch.org/resources/all-things-are-new/content/topic/how_can_i_pray_effectively_all_things. What in this video stood out the most?

3. Ask group members to keep a prayer journal for a period of time, recording when and how they prayed and any personal observations, including God's responses. Share insights gleaned from the journals during a group meeting.

4. Discuss any changes you'd like to make in your practice of prayer. Commit to hold one another accountable, perhaps by checking in regularly with a prayer partner. At the end of six months or a year, evaluate as a group how your prayer lives have been enriched.